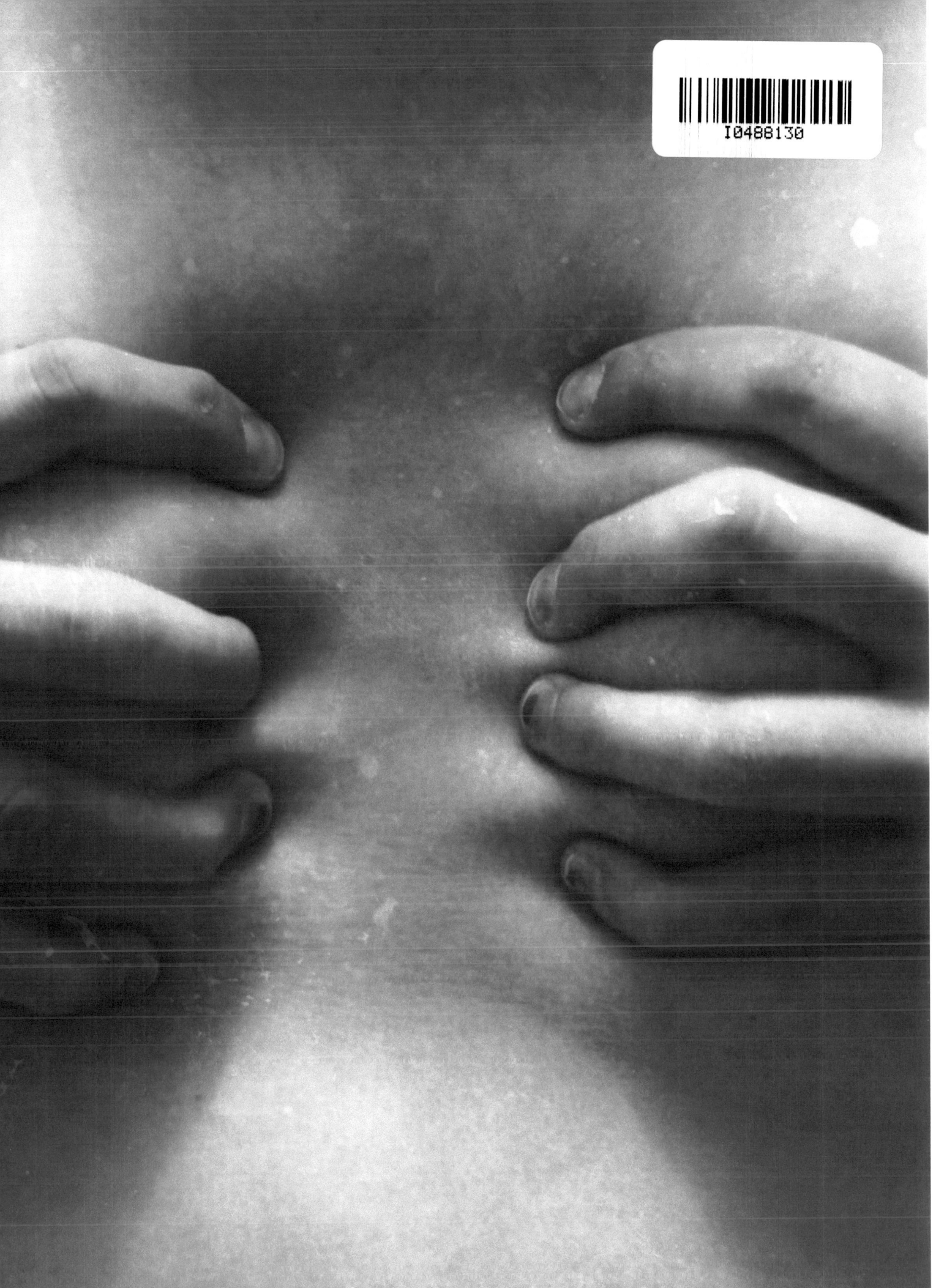

# FLEETING BRAINWAVES & MIND COCKTAILS: ALICE IN HER WONDERLAND

## SISSORELLE FEROX

This is a book of mysteries of my head, realized through a long process of pulling out various mind cocktails, fleeting brainwaves, and half baked ideas. Whatever that happened to flow and ebb from the mindwater emptying out onto the reality before me is what ended up here. This is not well curated, nor is it a master-crafted. It just astream of what exists between me and you; this is a flow of consciousness from me to you. In order to achieve my thoughts withsome amount of clarity, I've only been able to put that task to the one person I know best: myself. This is a book of self portraits and mashups intertwined with brain signals and bits of my aura captured through photography.

My work is loosely photographic, taking the form of prints, digital images, and multi-sensory media using experimental techniques and unconventional digital and physical materials. Its subject is often taken from the phenomena of the cyber-verse. I use photographic manipulation to produce an encounter that reflects a recognition of an increasingly mitigated physical experience of the world. My work combines delusional reality with physically graphic realism that explores the dark side of the human experience in the physical and intangible realms of our environment and beyond.

The figure is the forte ahnd crown of my manipulations; I unabashedly use it as an anchor to examine topics ranging from what defines our humanity, artificial consciousness, and a conjoined self-thought that plague our inner voices.

While the cyber-verse is a constant focus for myself; more recently, a consistent spice of obsessive self-dissection and examination has emerged in my practice. This dissection of the self has evolved into an examination of other individuals. A library of people, or specimens has accumulated and has begun to excite me in new ways and influence the grand architecture of my practice.

I can be contacted through number different mediums and I want to make those available to you, because I love you and really respect your choice to read this book. It means a lot to me.

http://sissorelle.com
https://www.facebook.com/Sissorelle
https://twitter.com/Sissorelle
http://sissorelle.tumblr.com
http://sissorelle.deviantart.com

A variety of fine art prints and other merchandise is available at my Society6 store: http://society6.com/sissorelleferox/

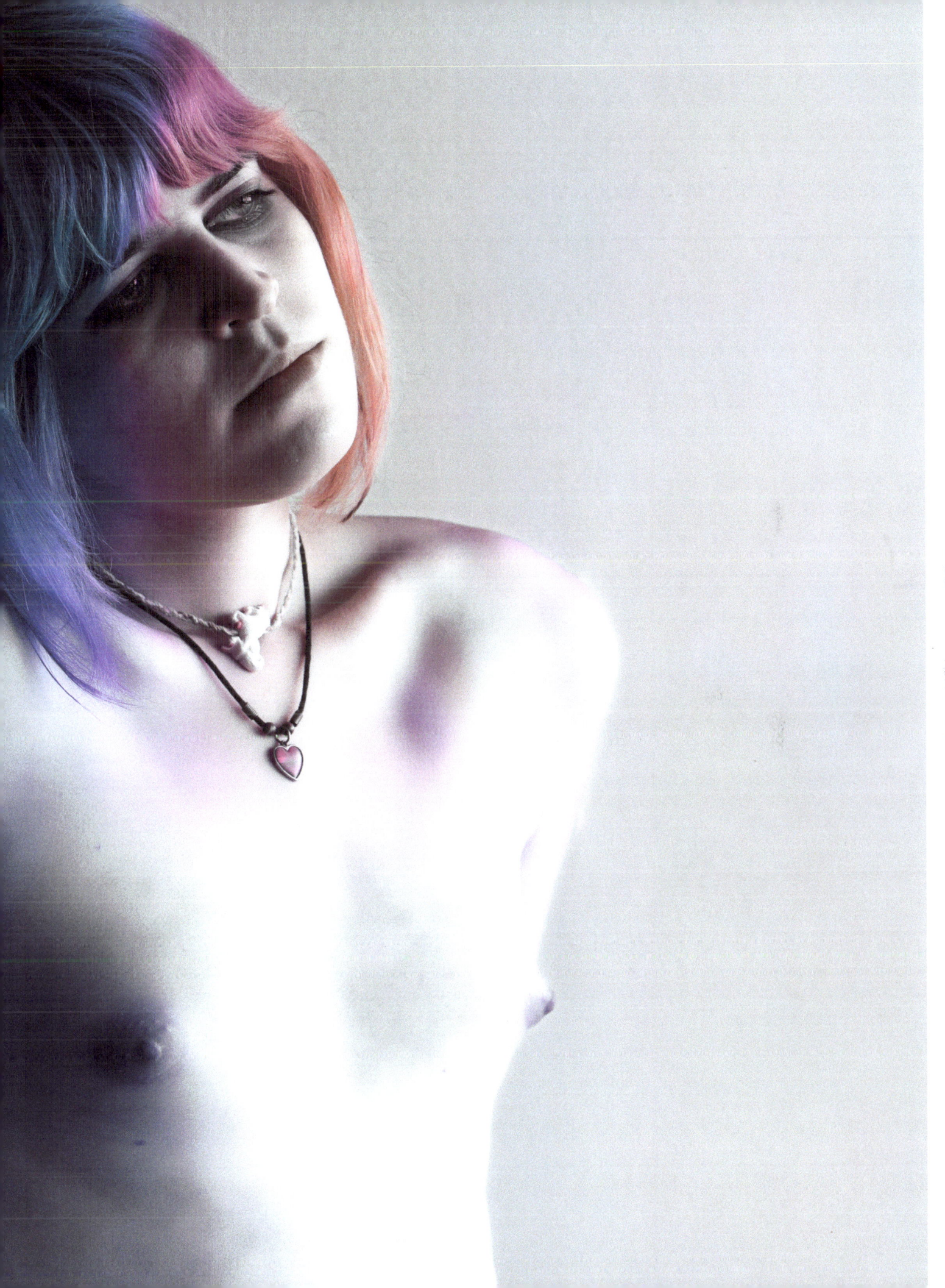

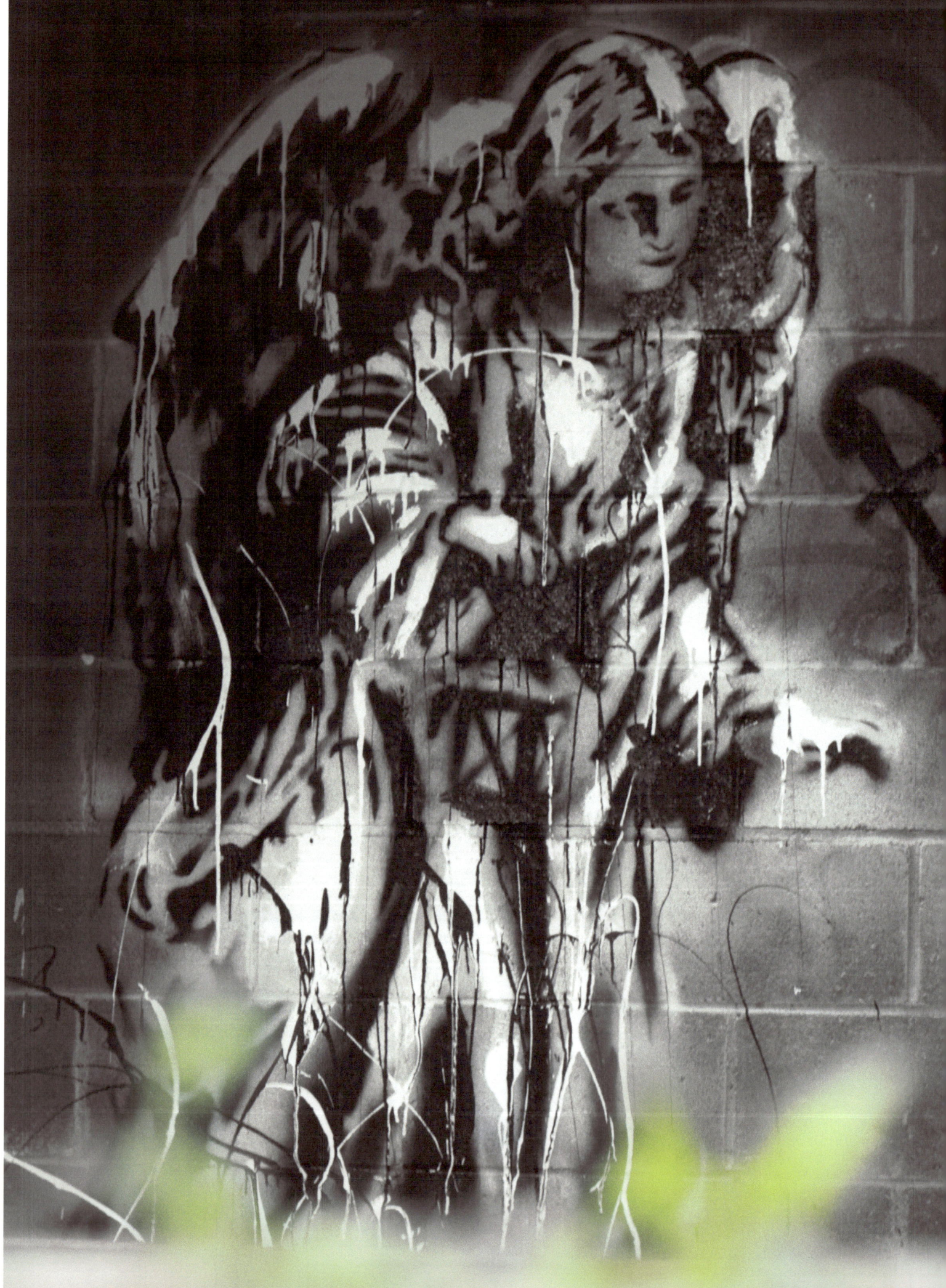

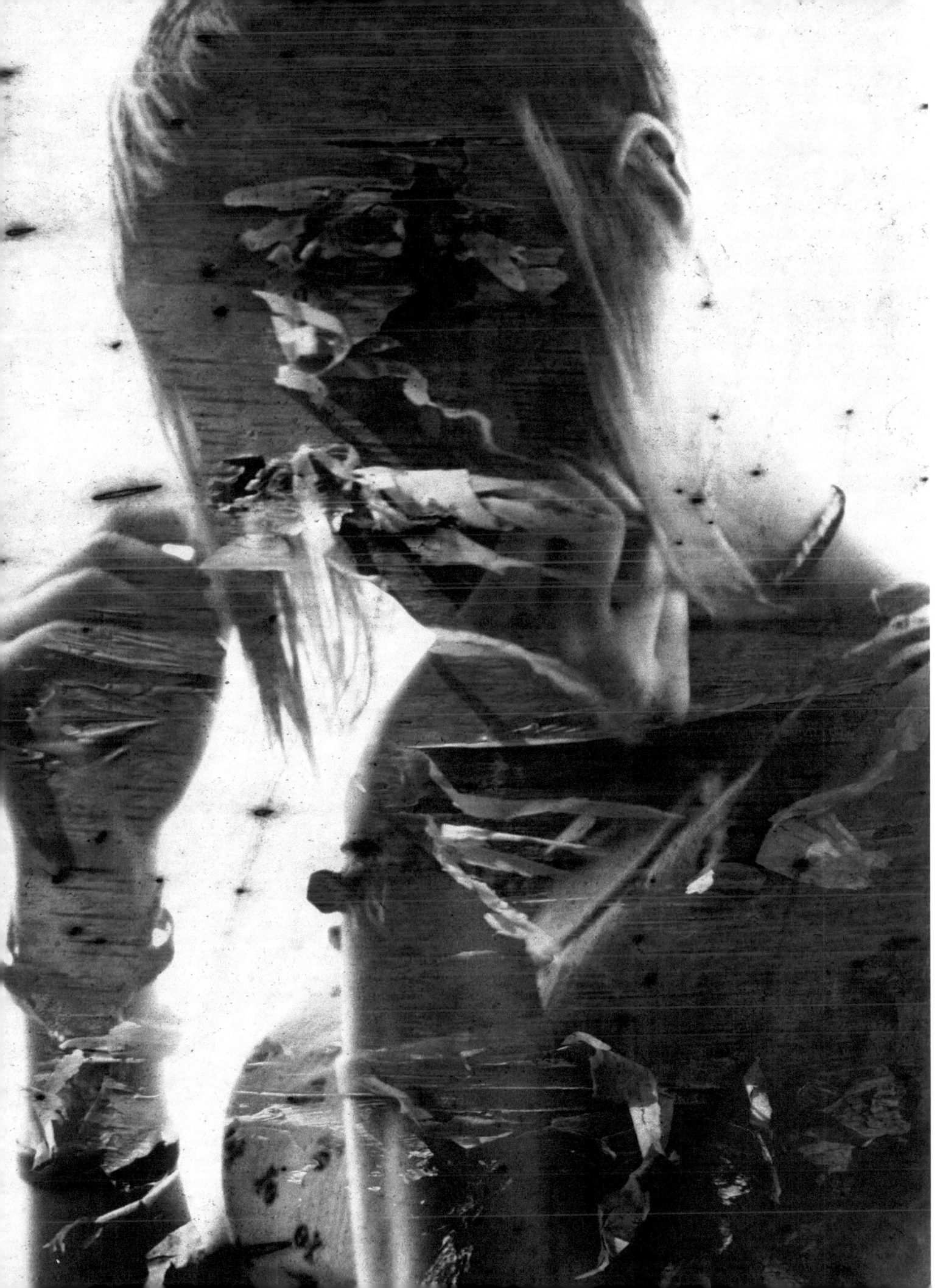

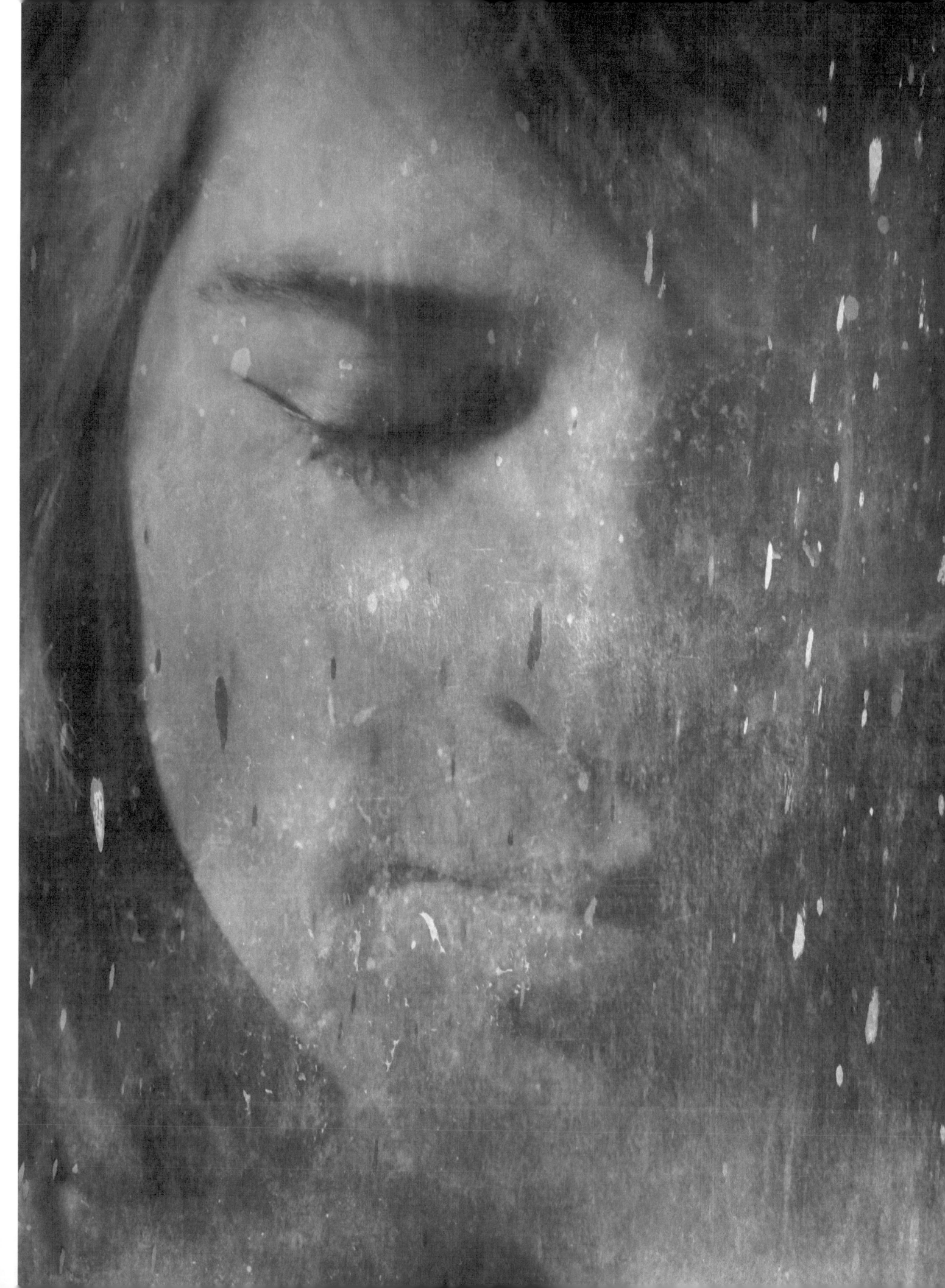

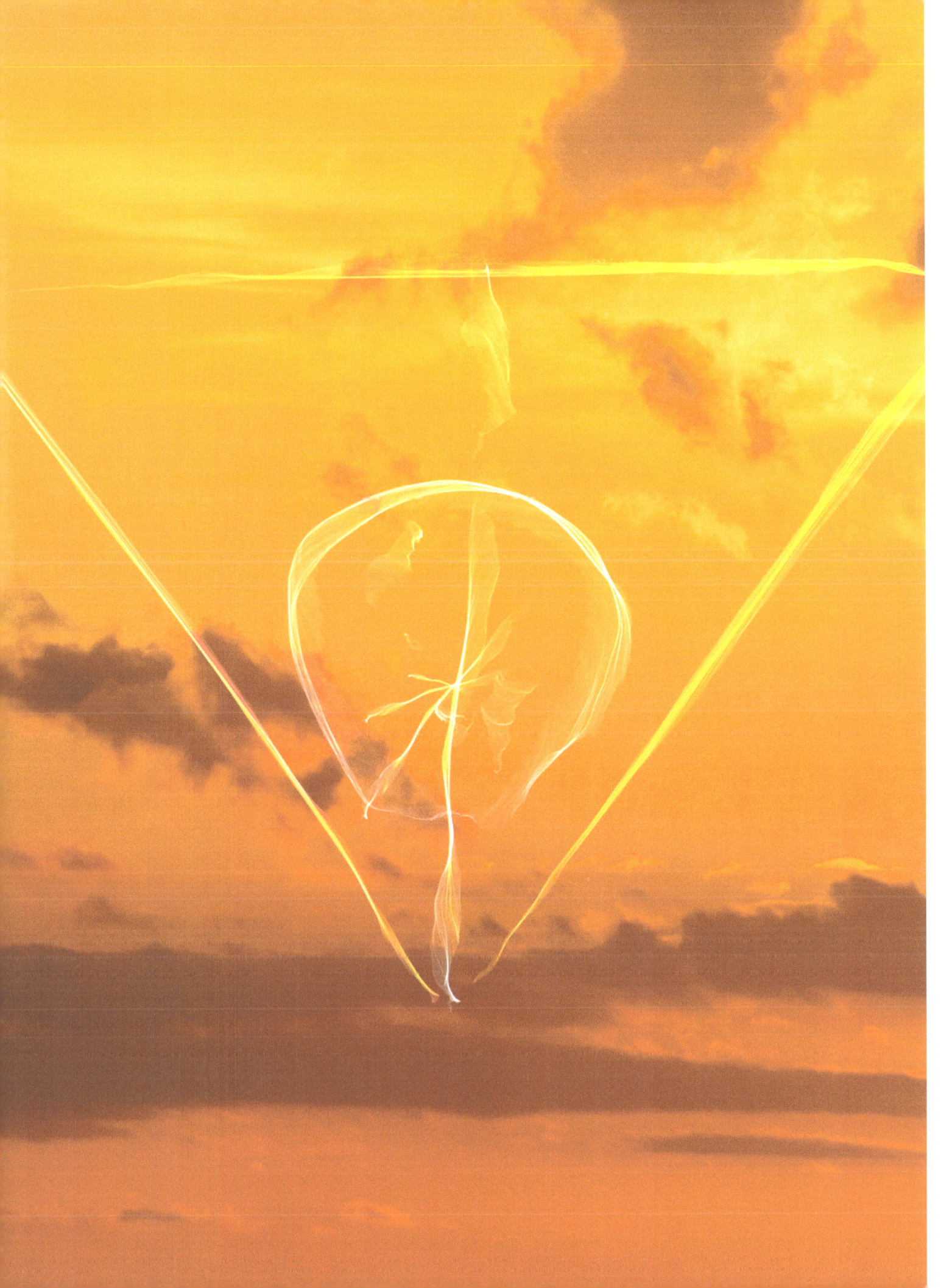

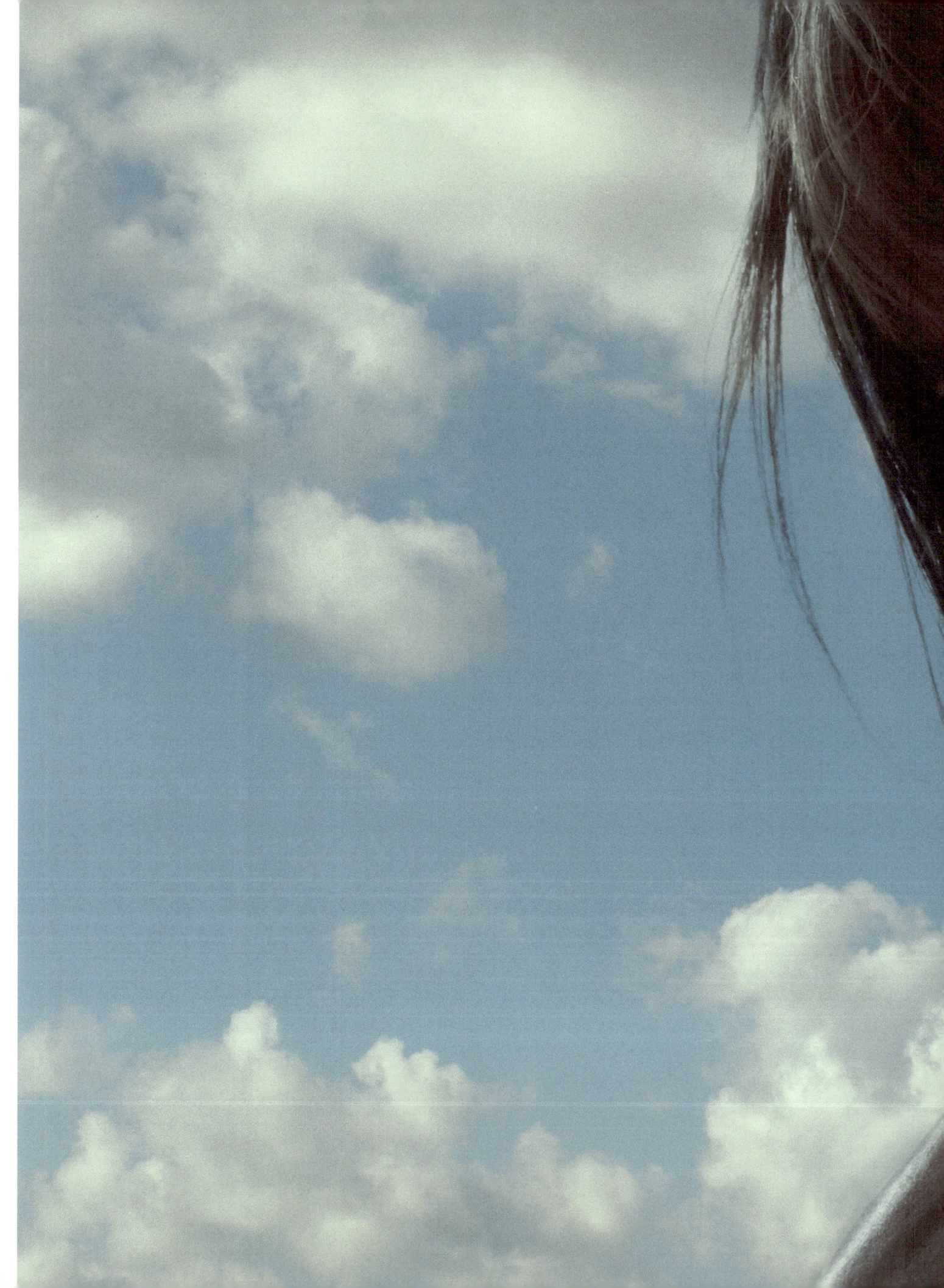

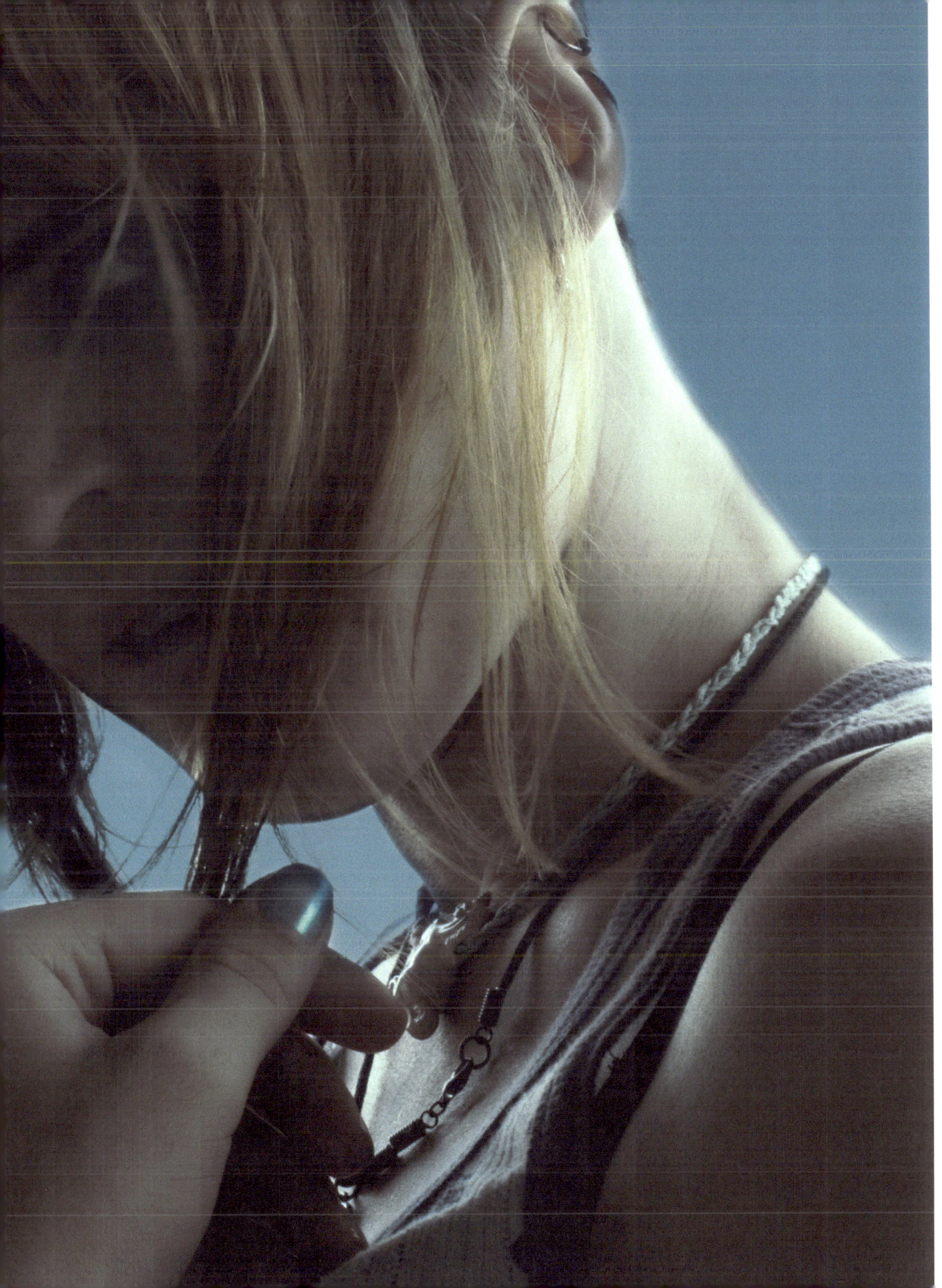

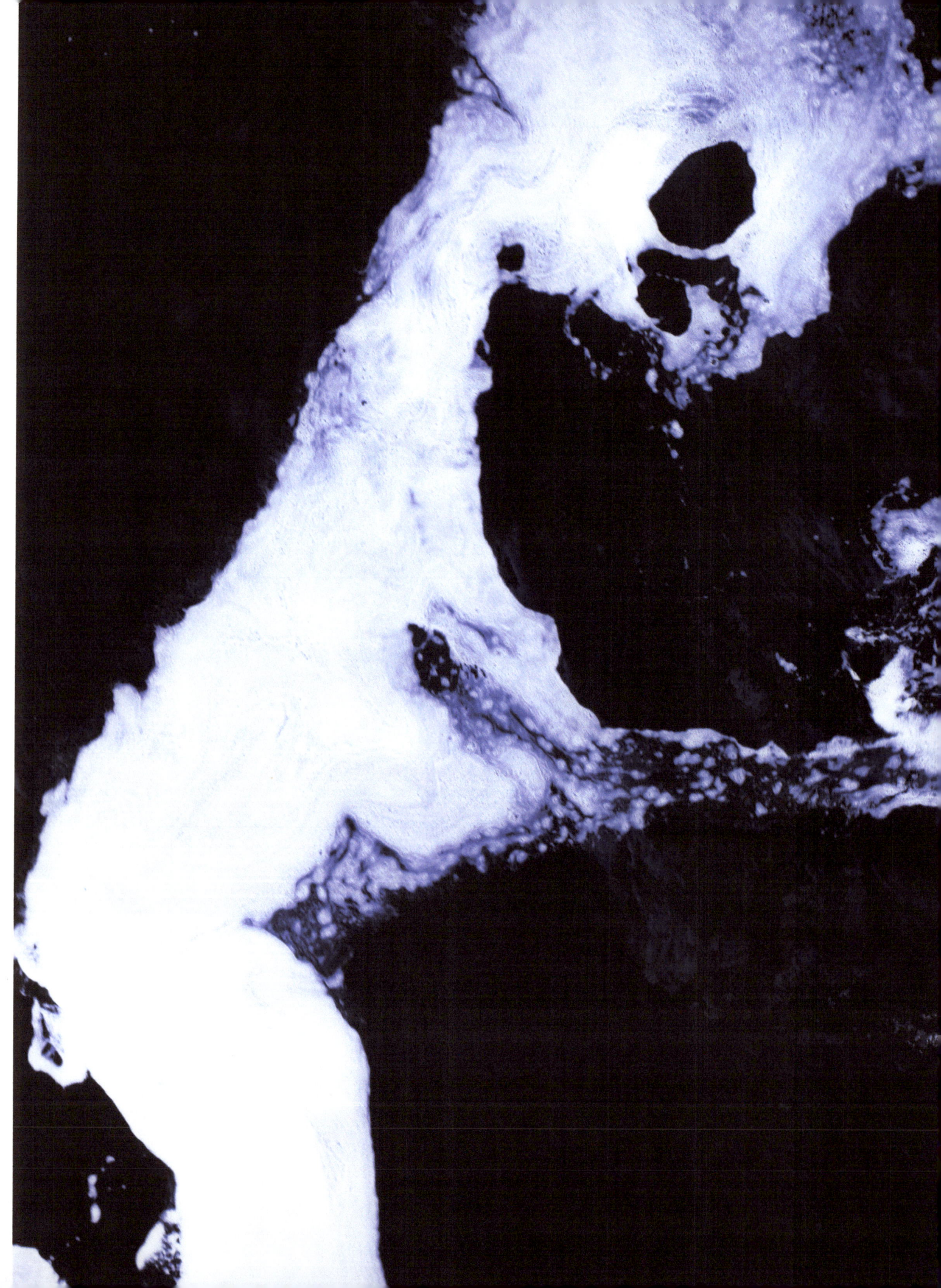

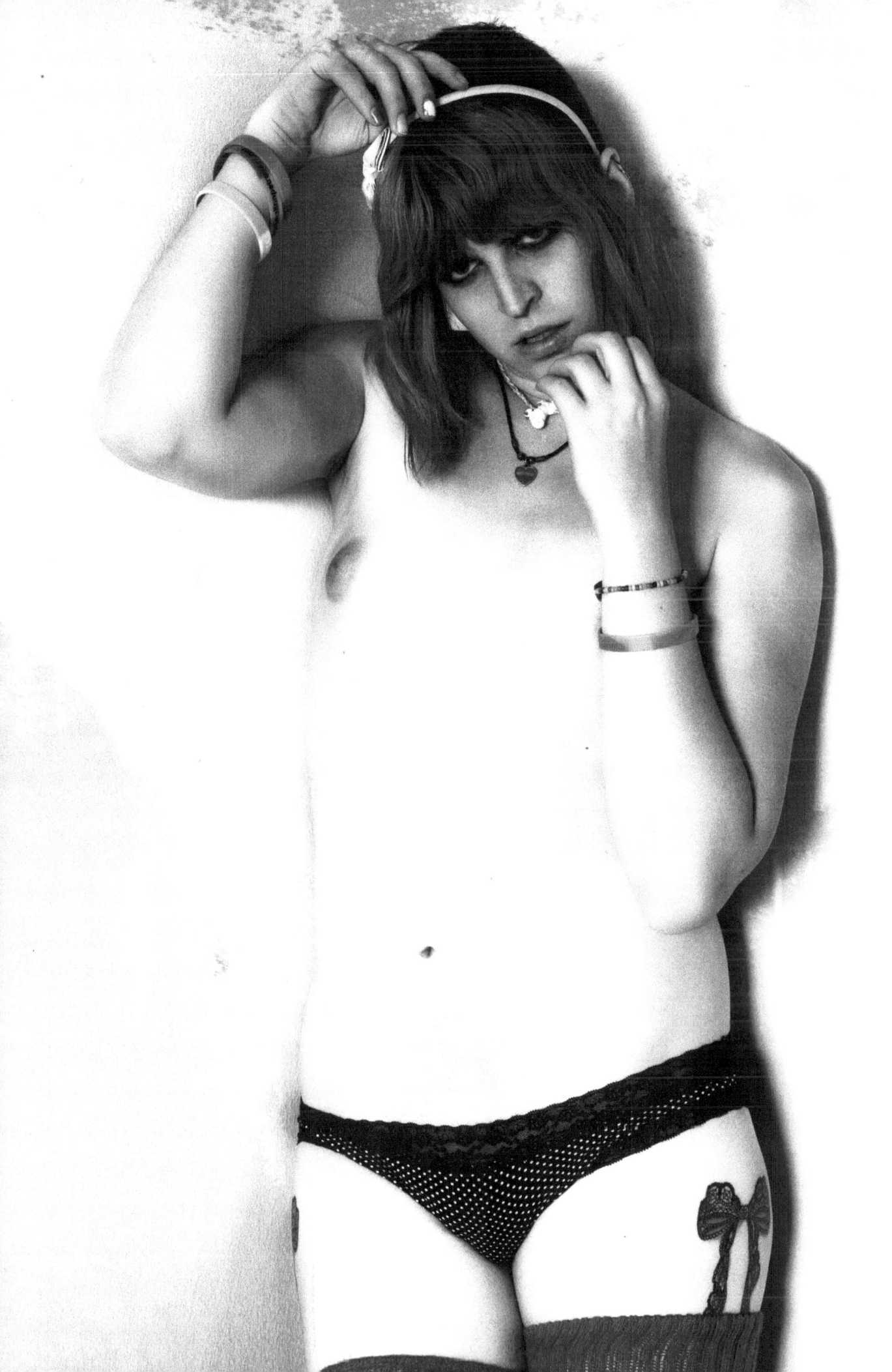

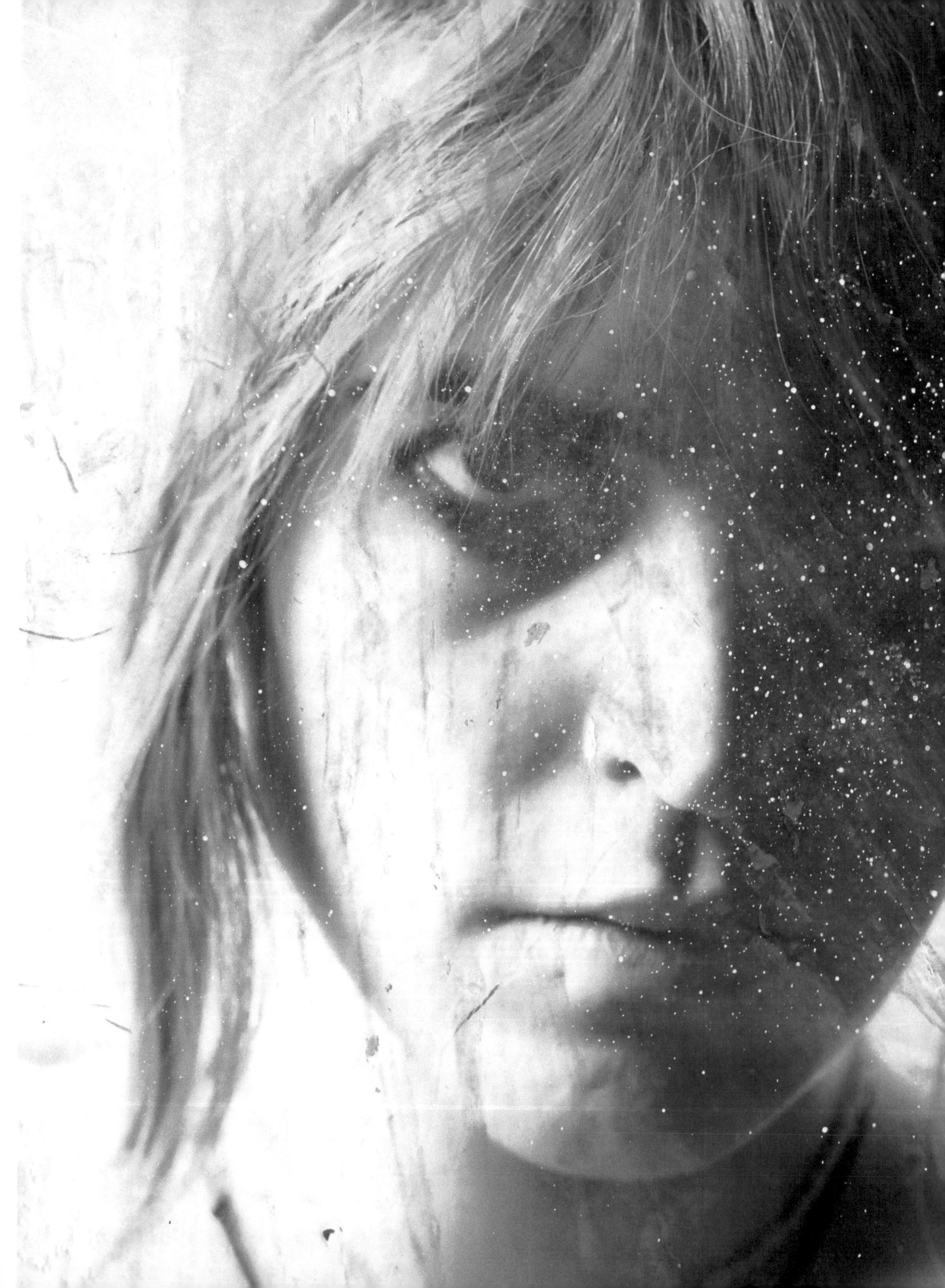

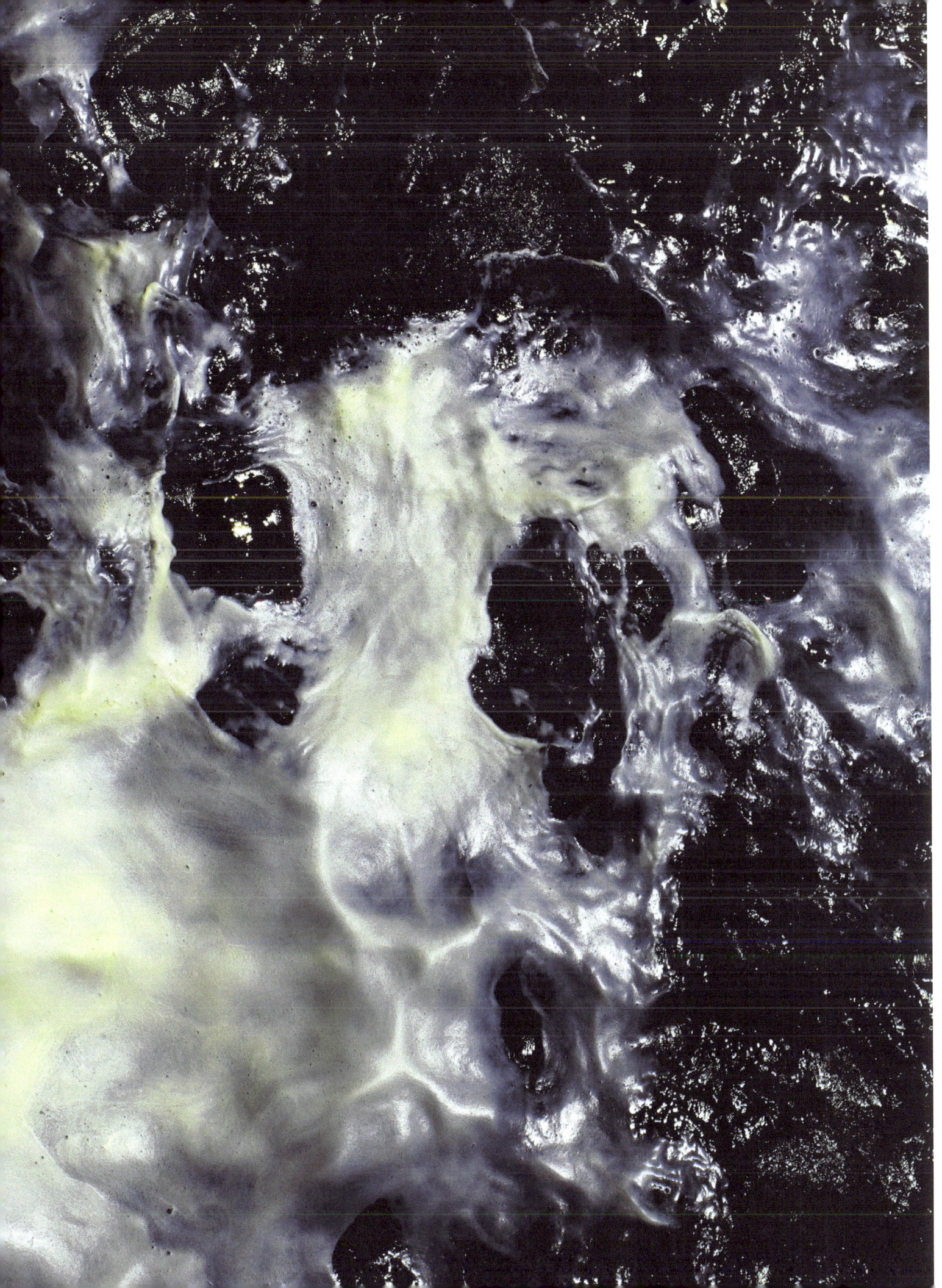

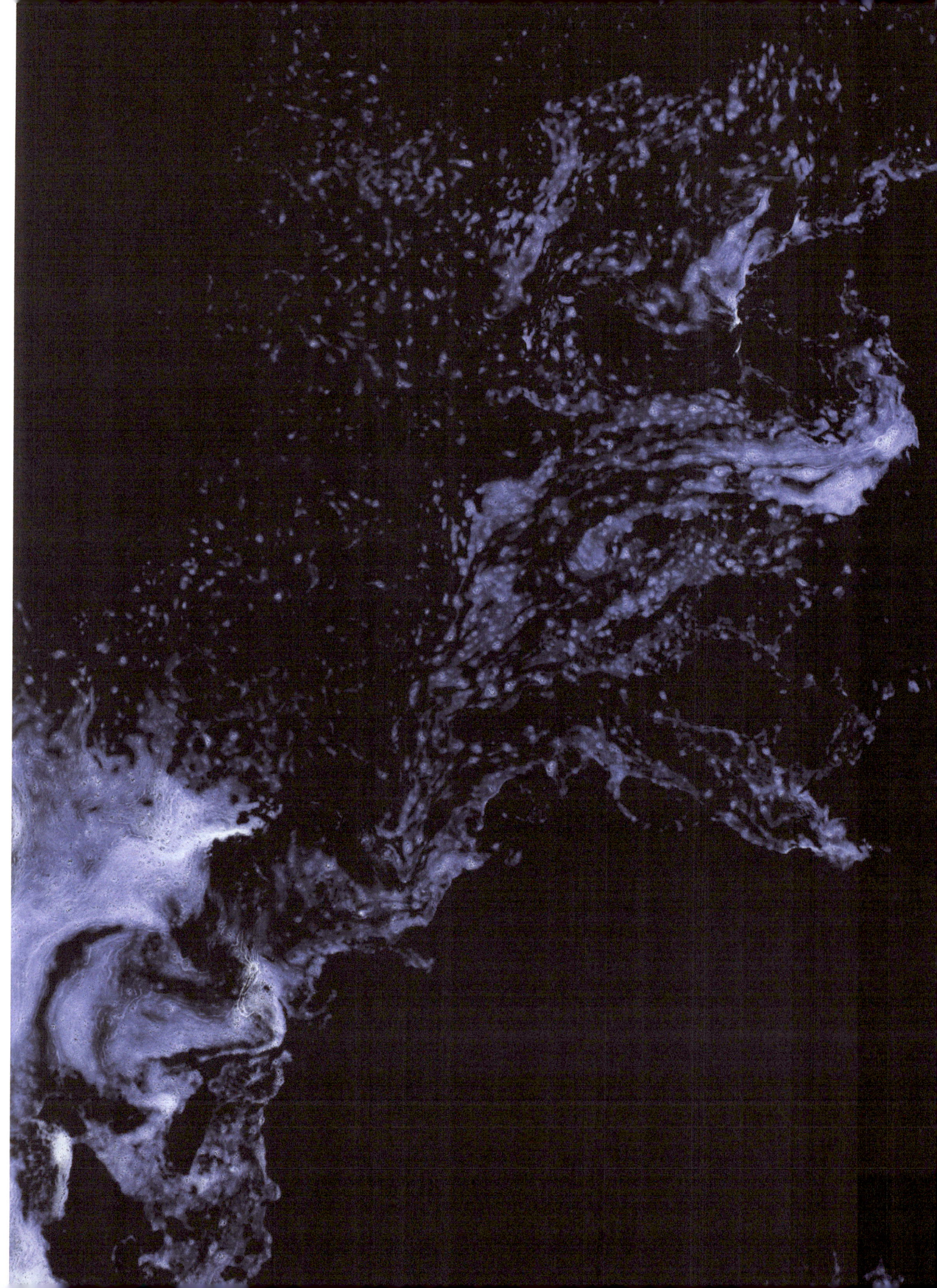

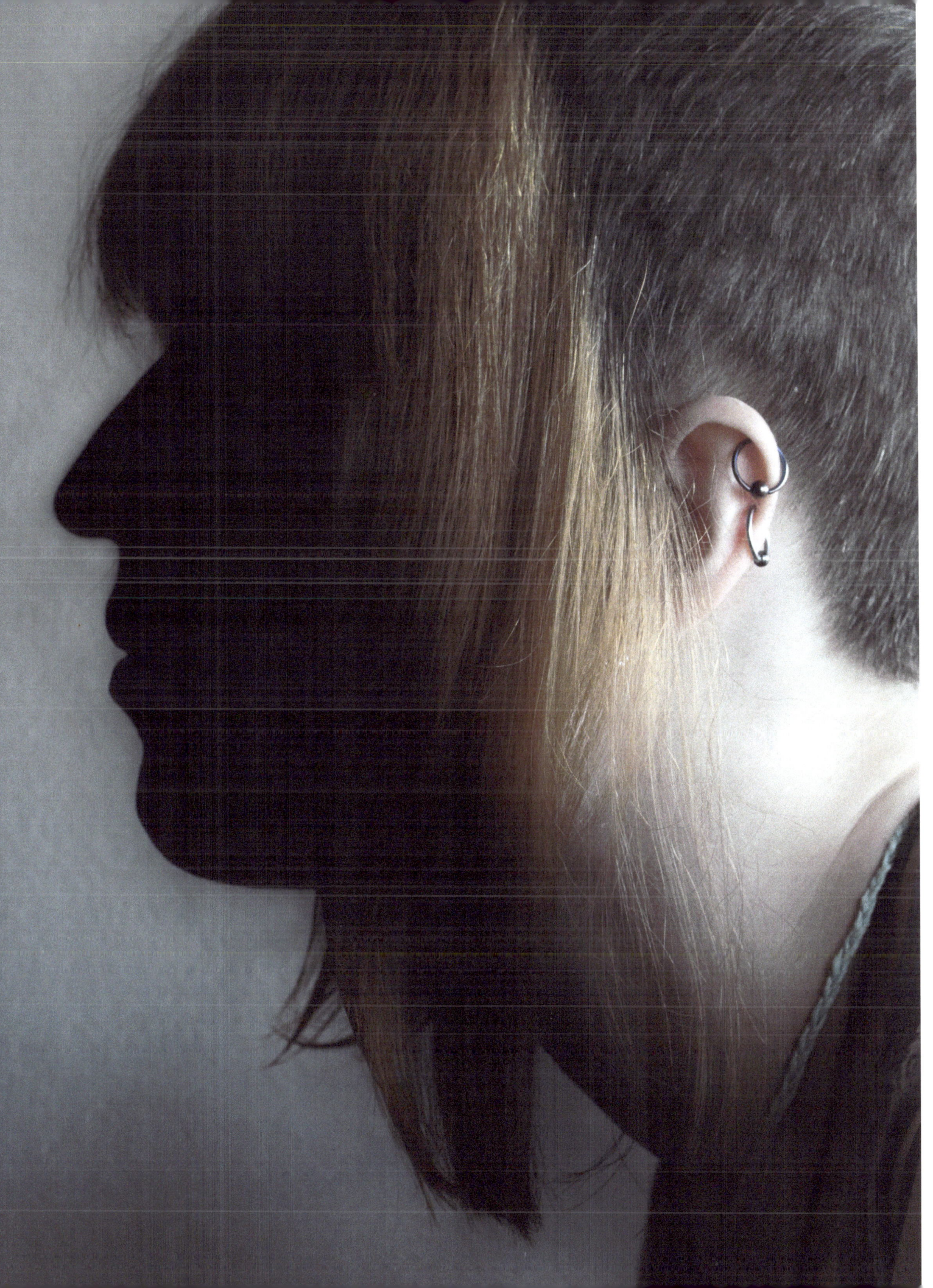

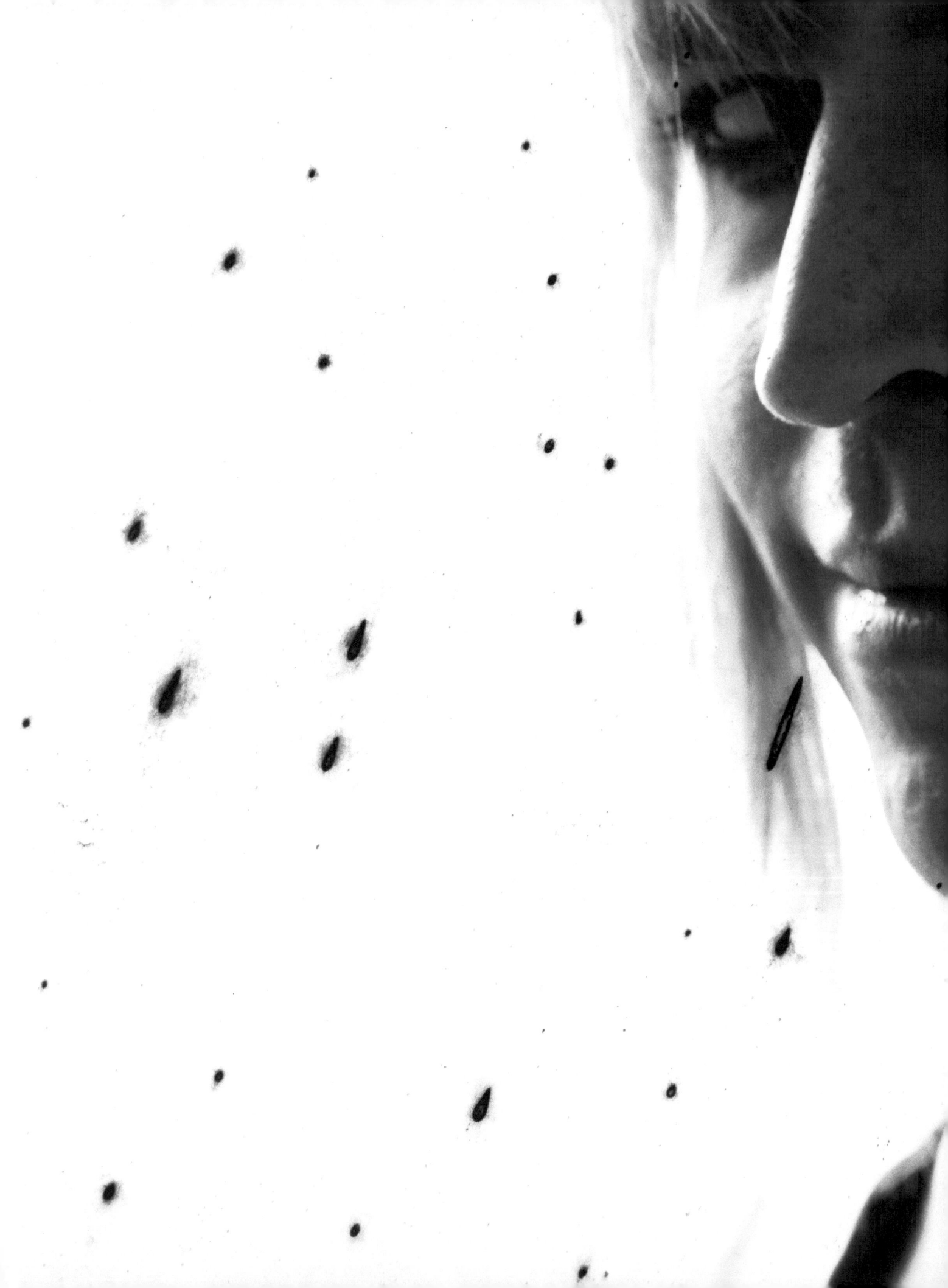

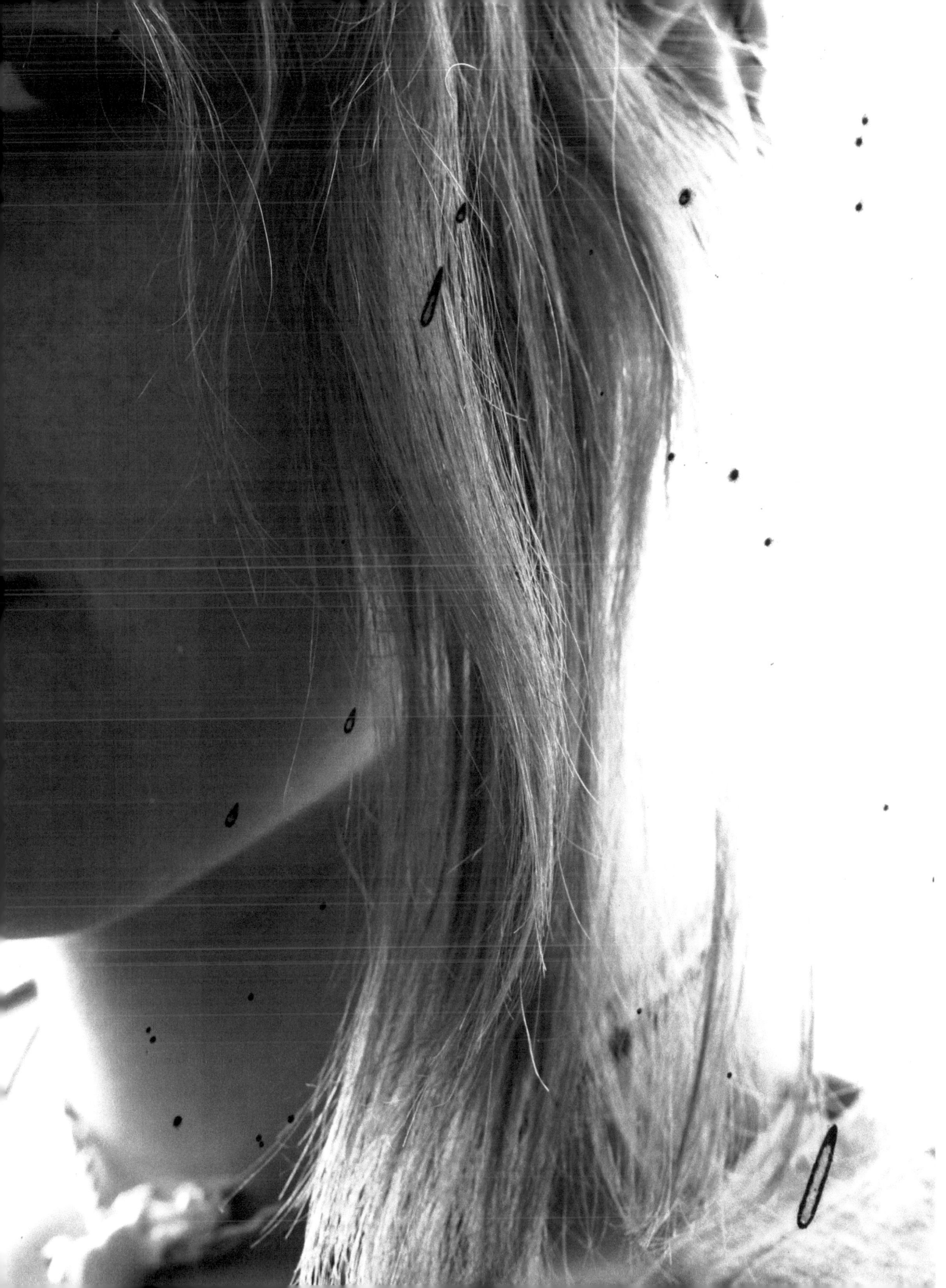

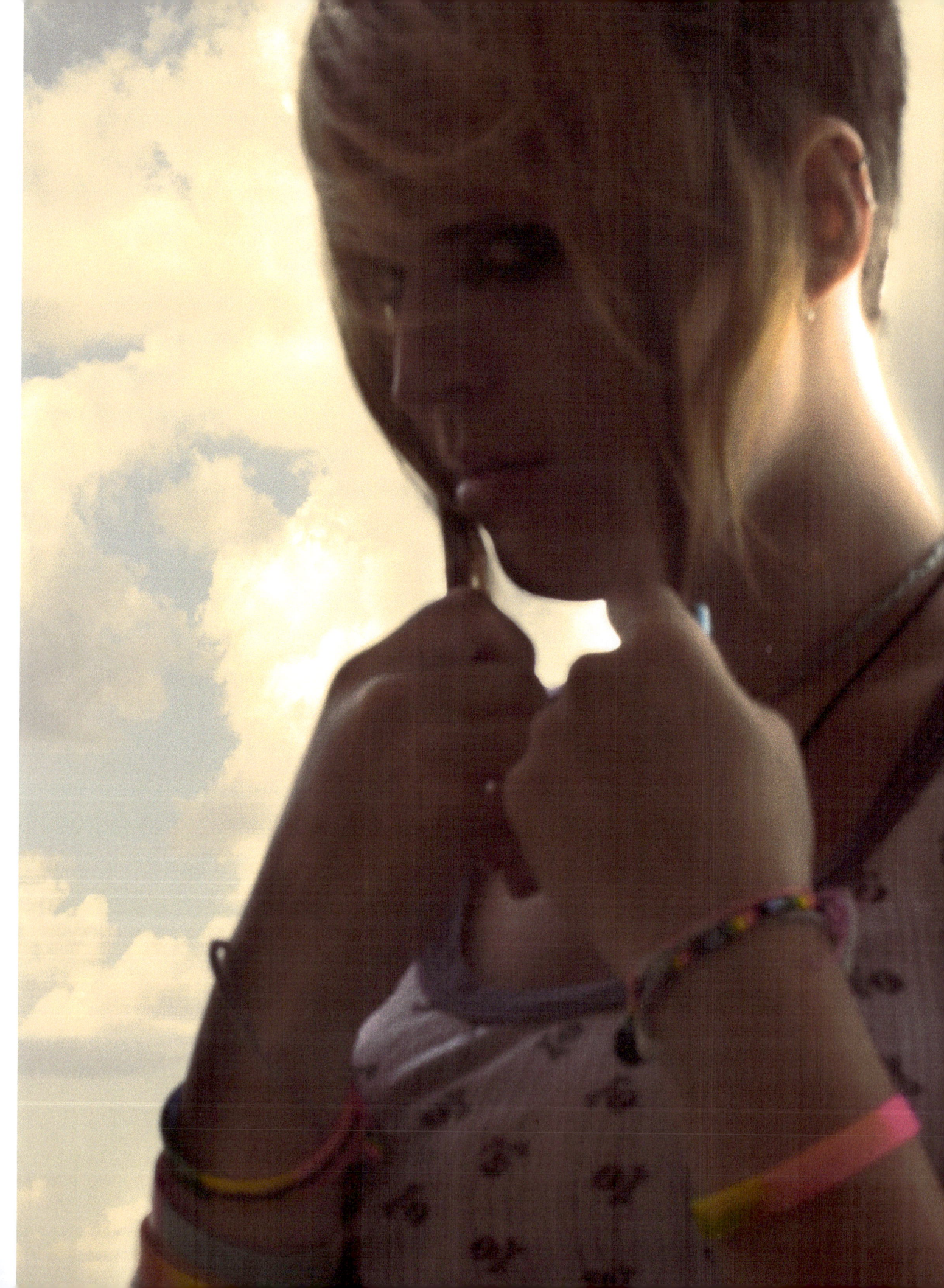

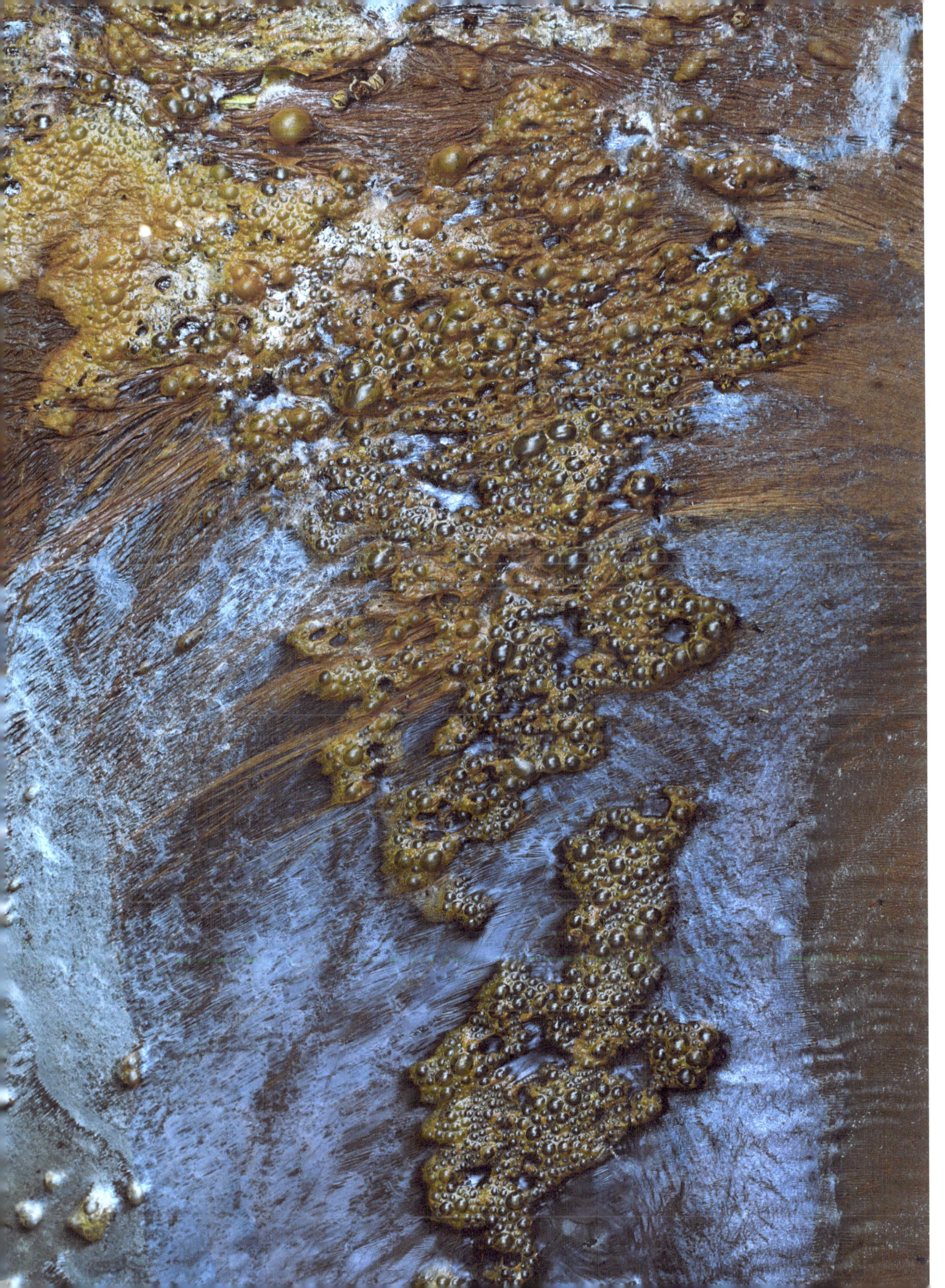

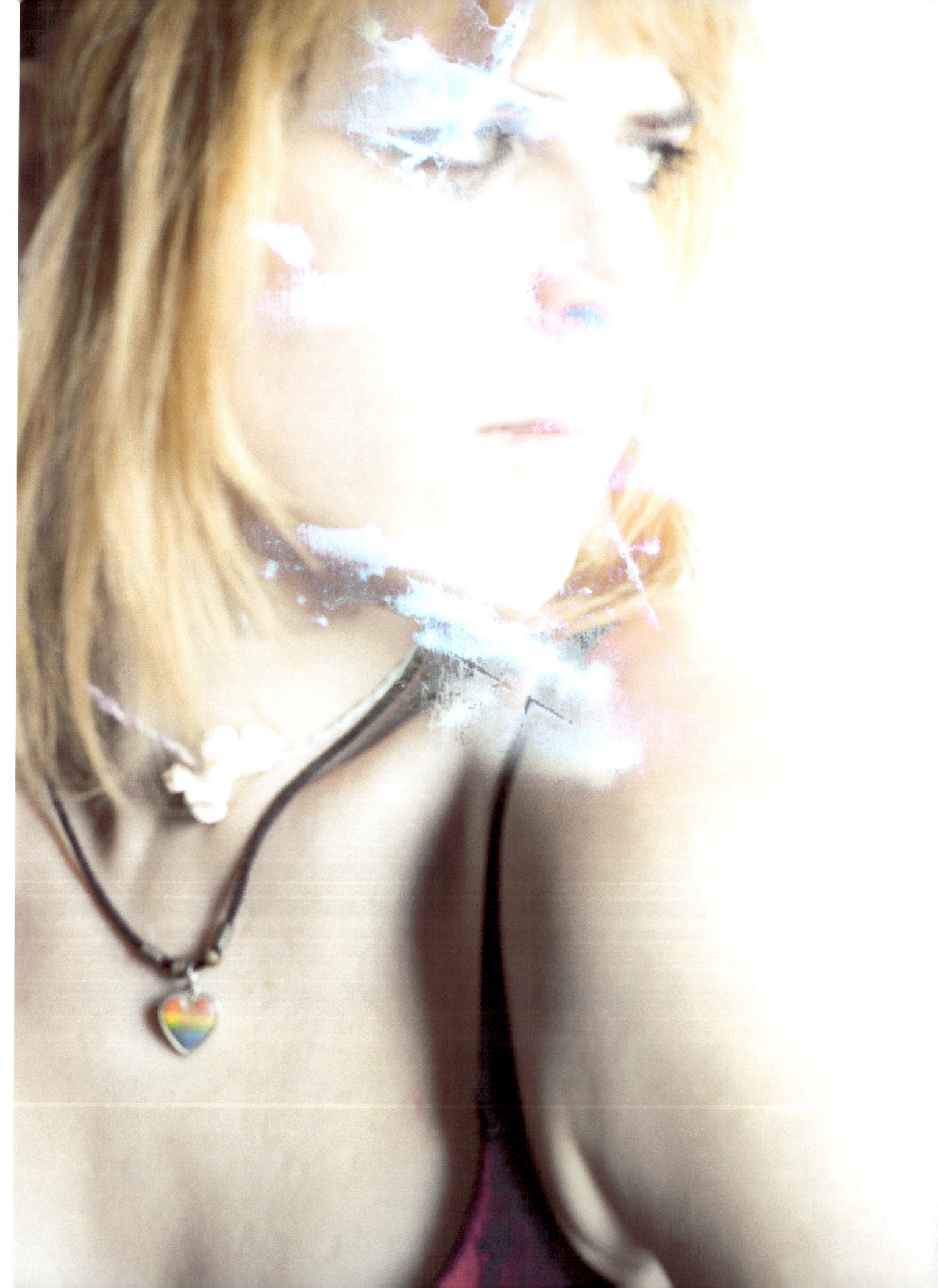

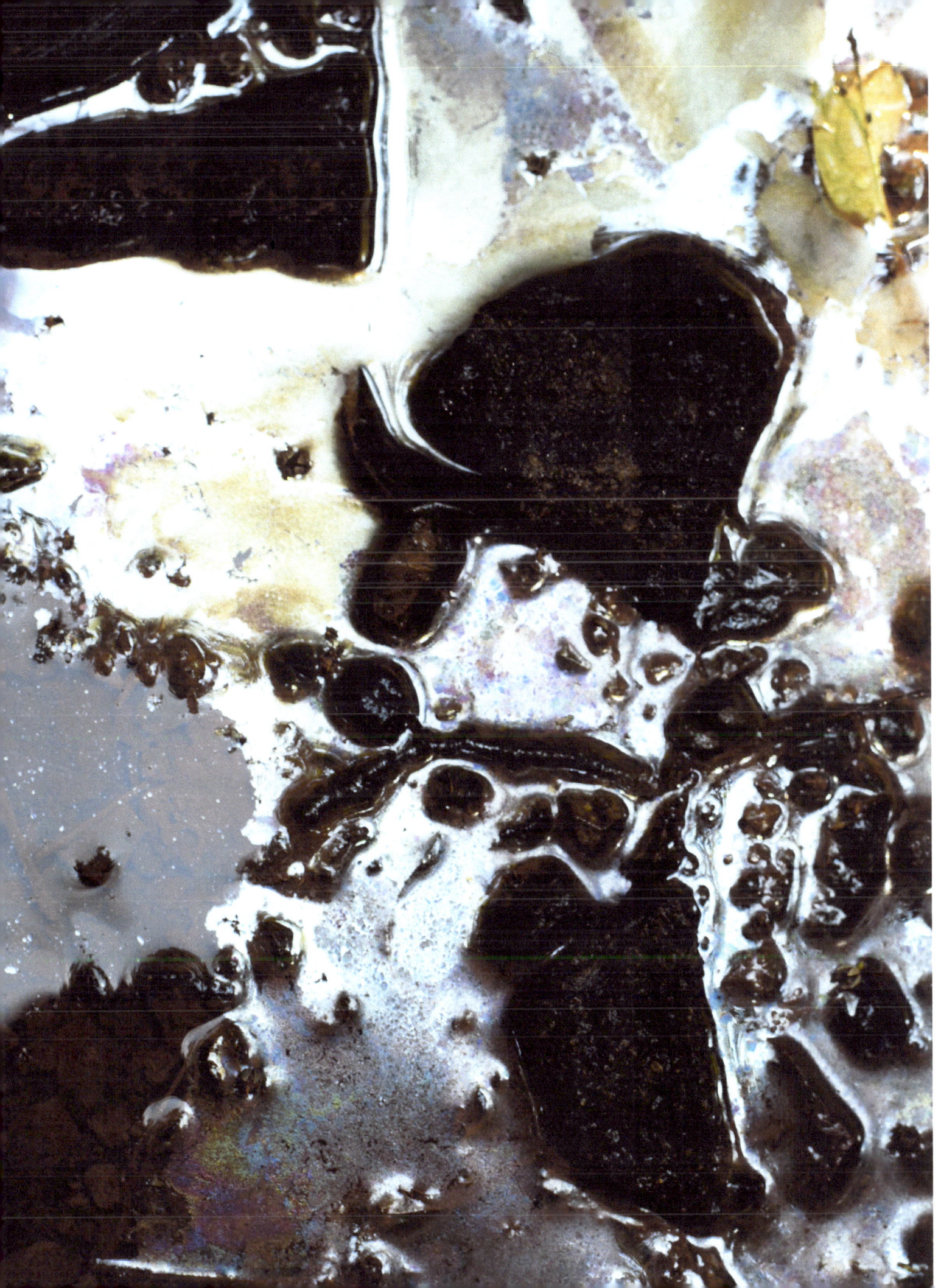

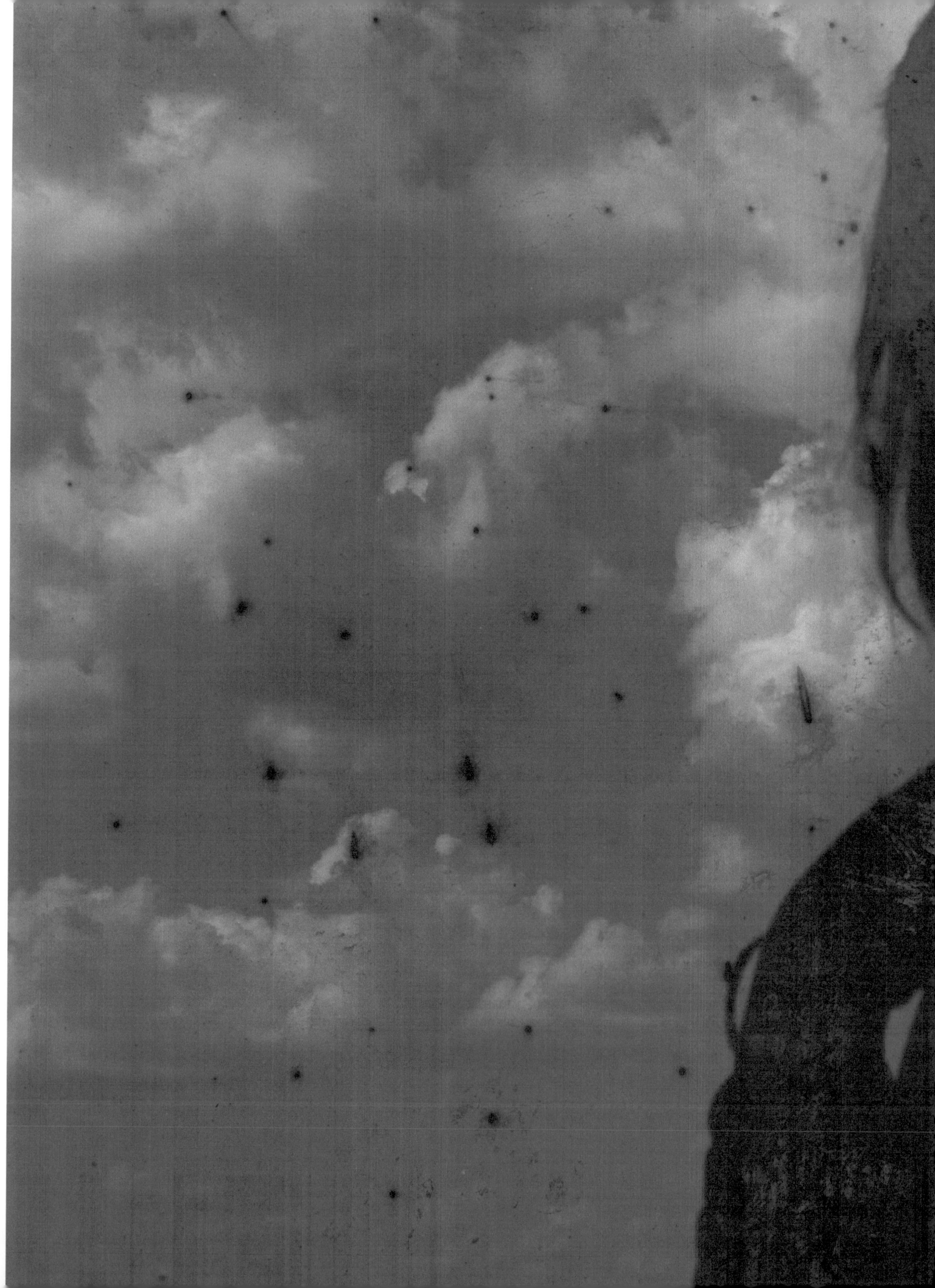

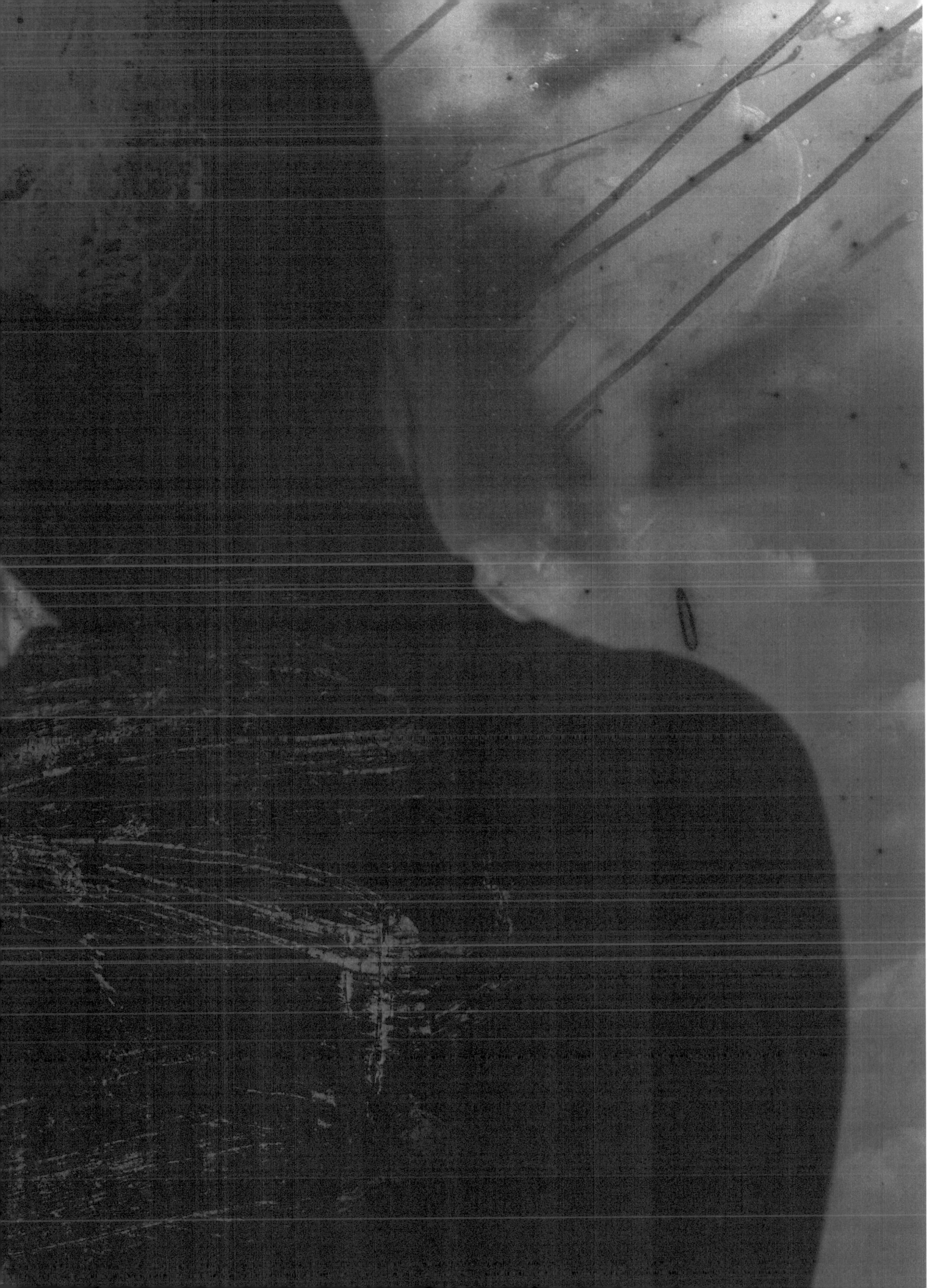

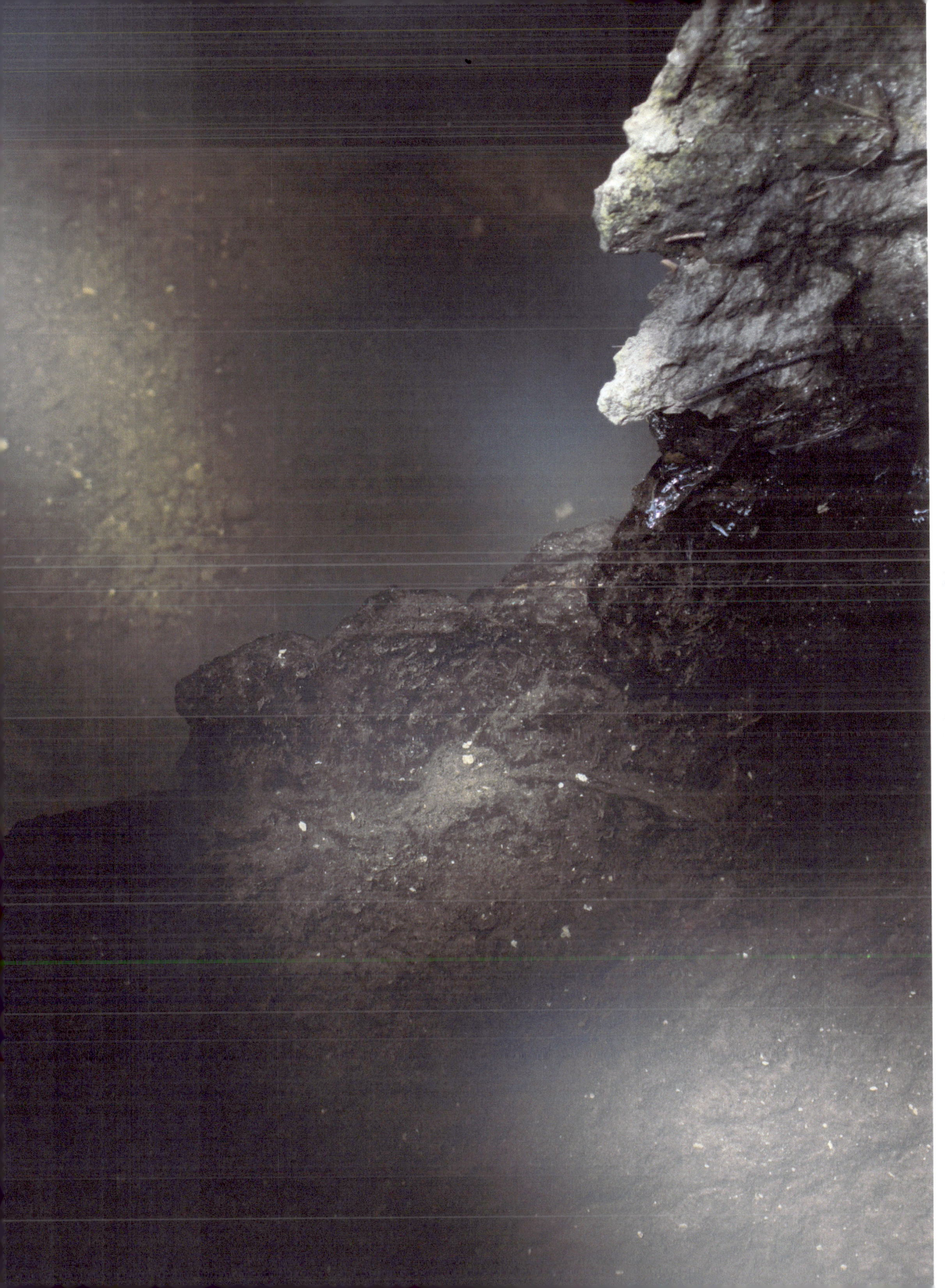

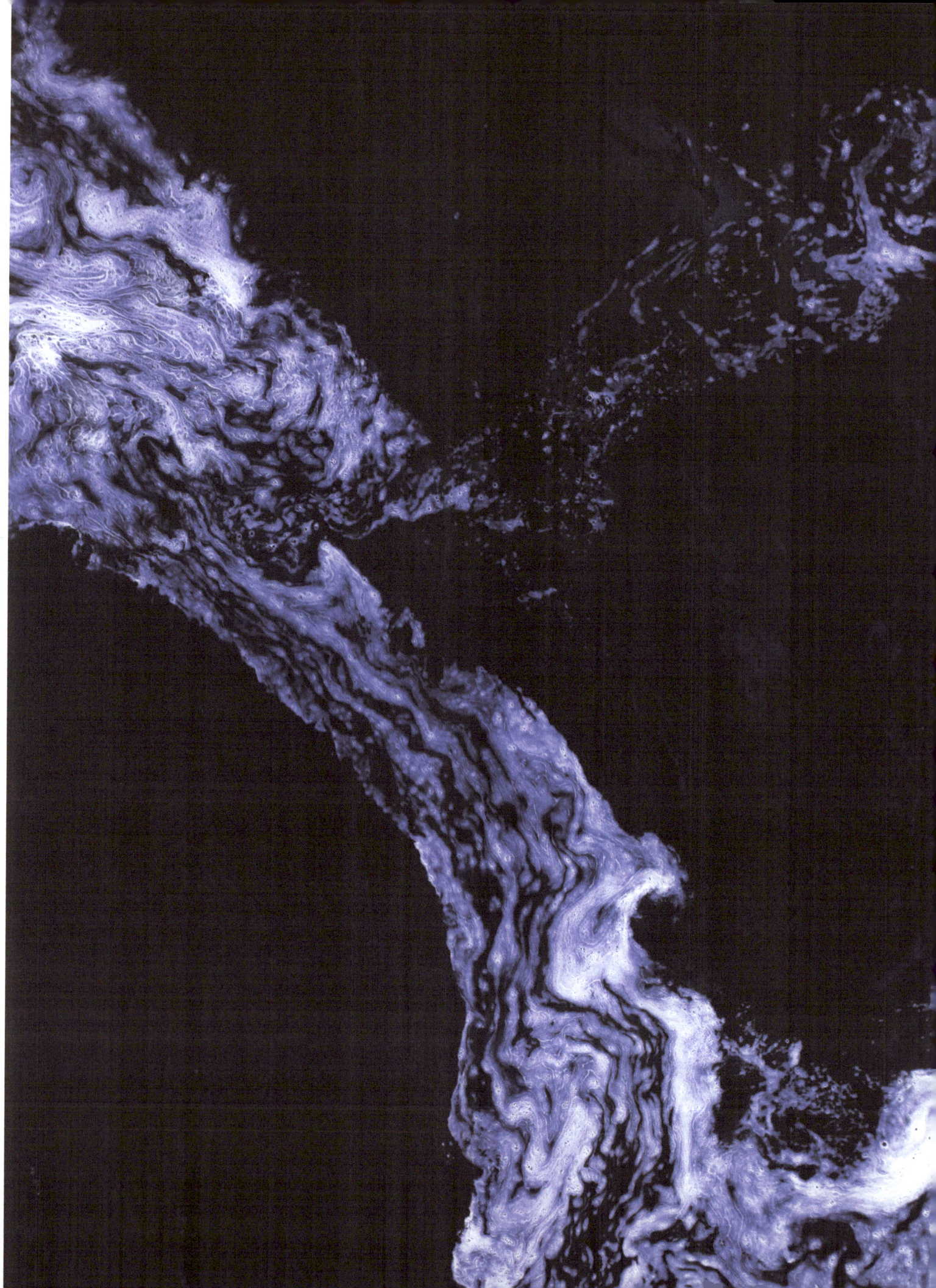

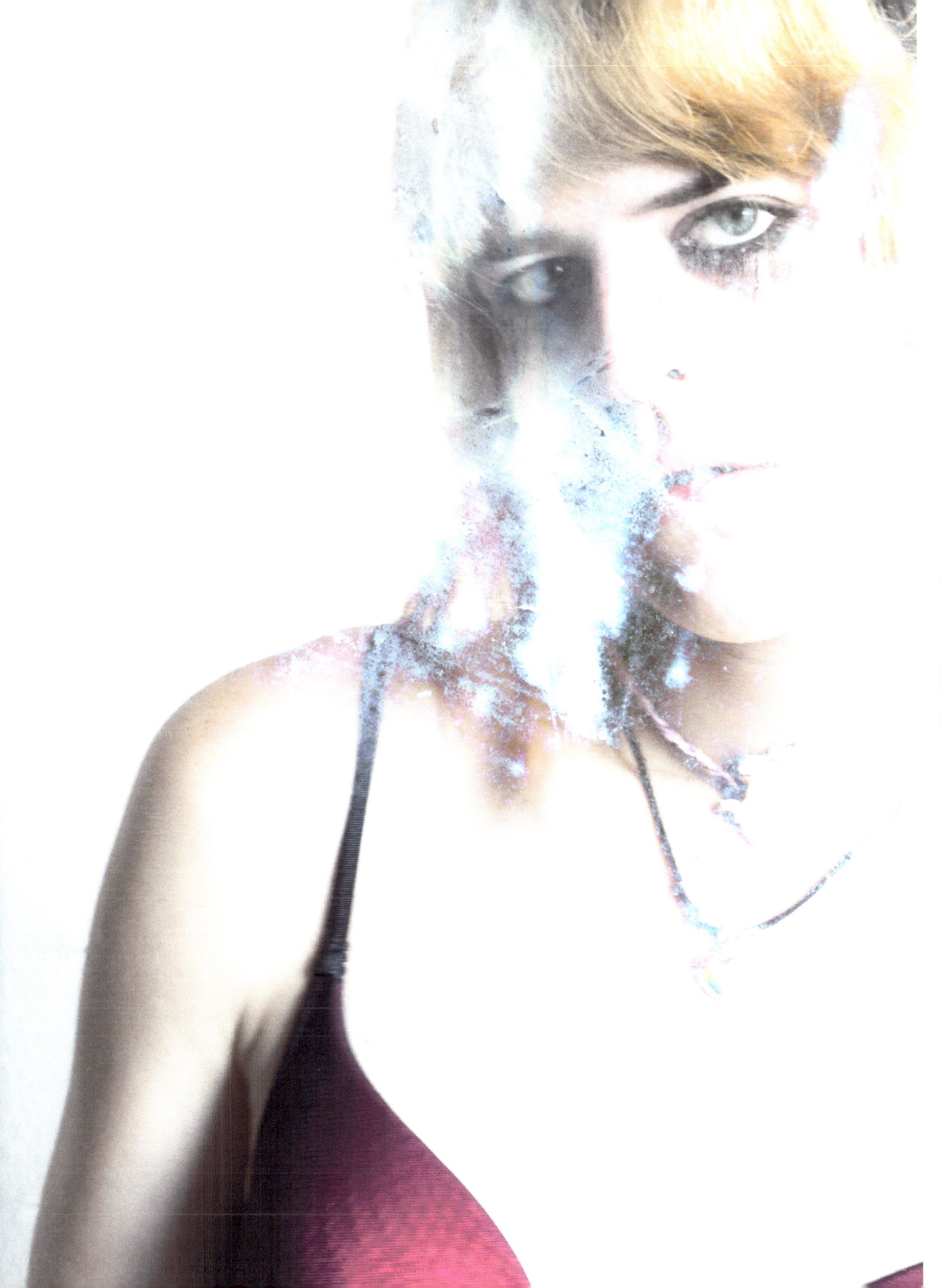

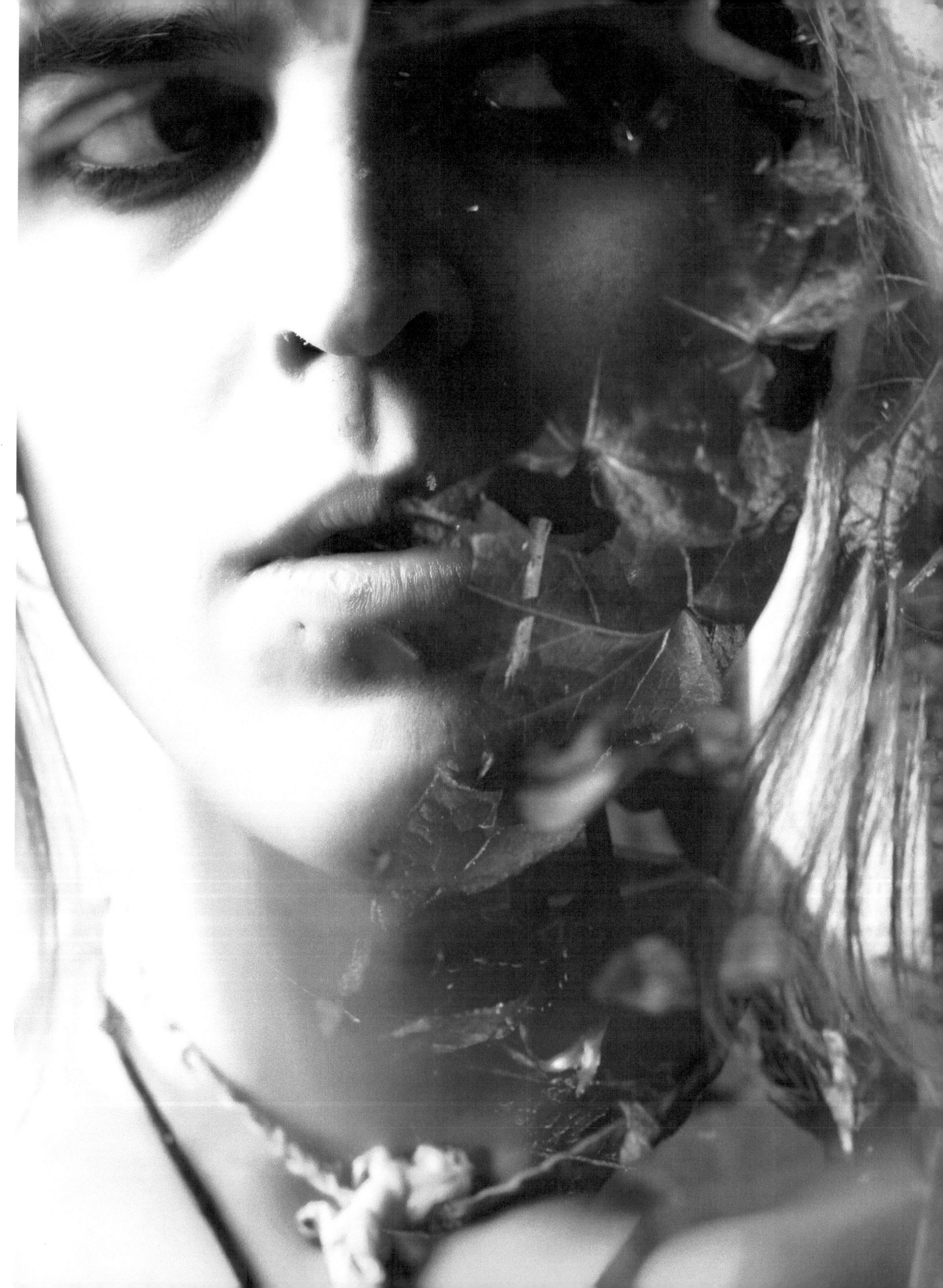

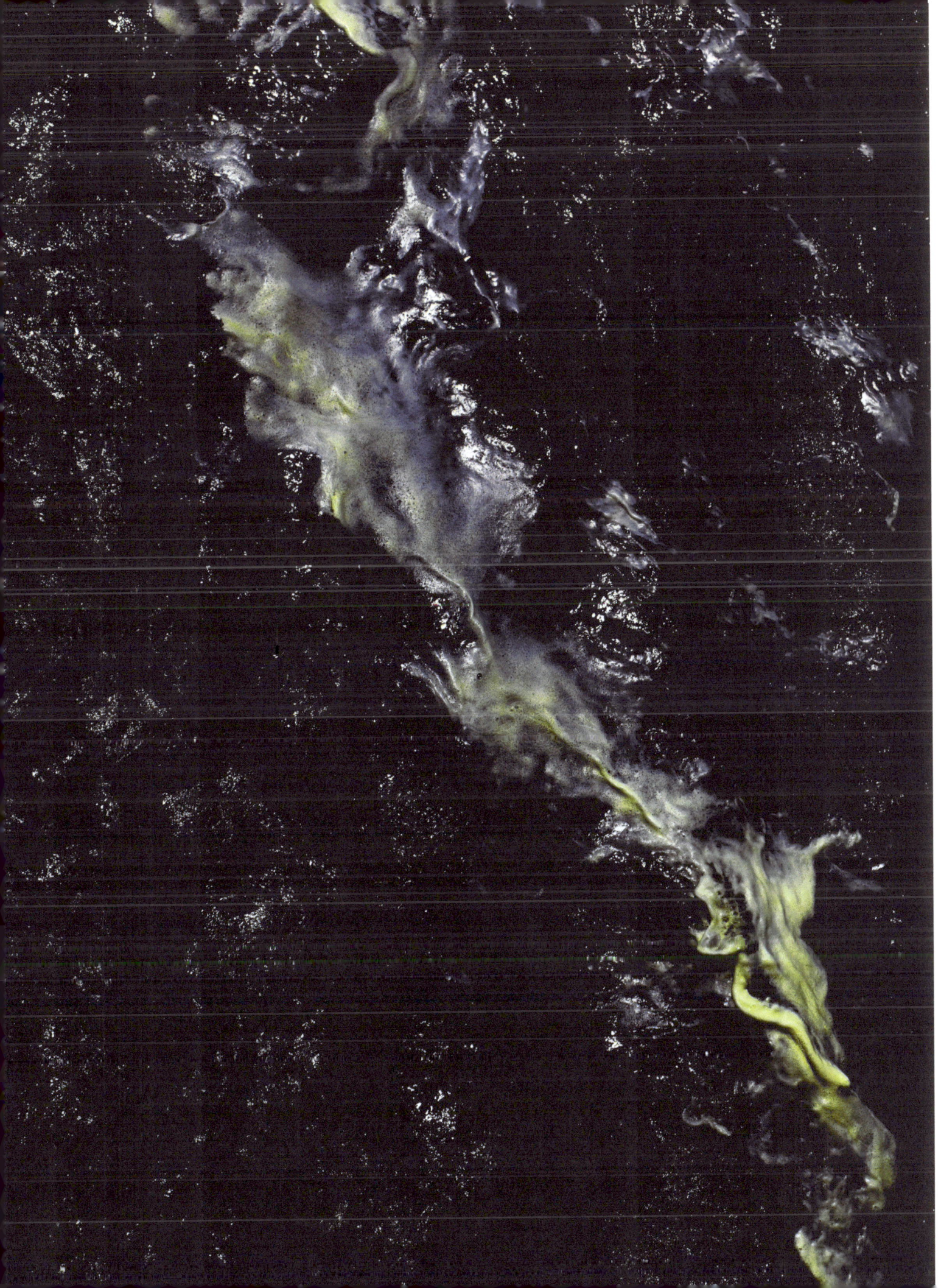

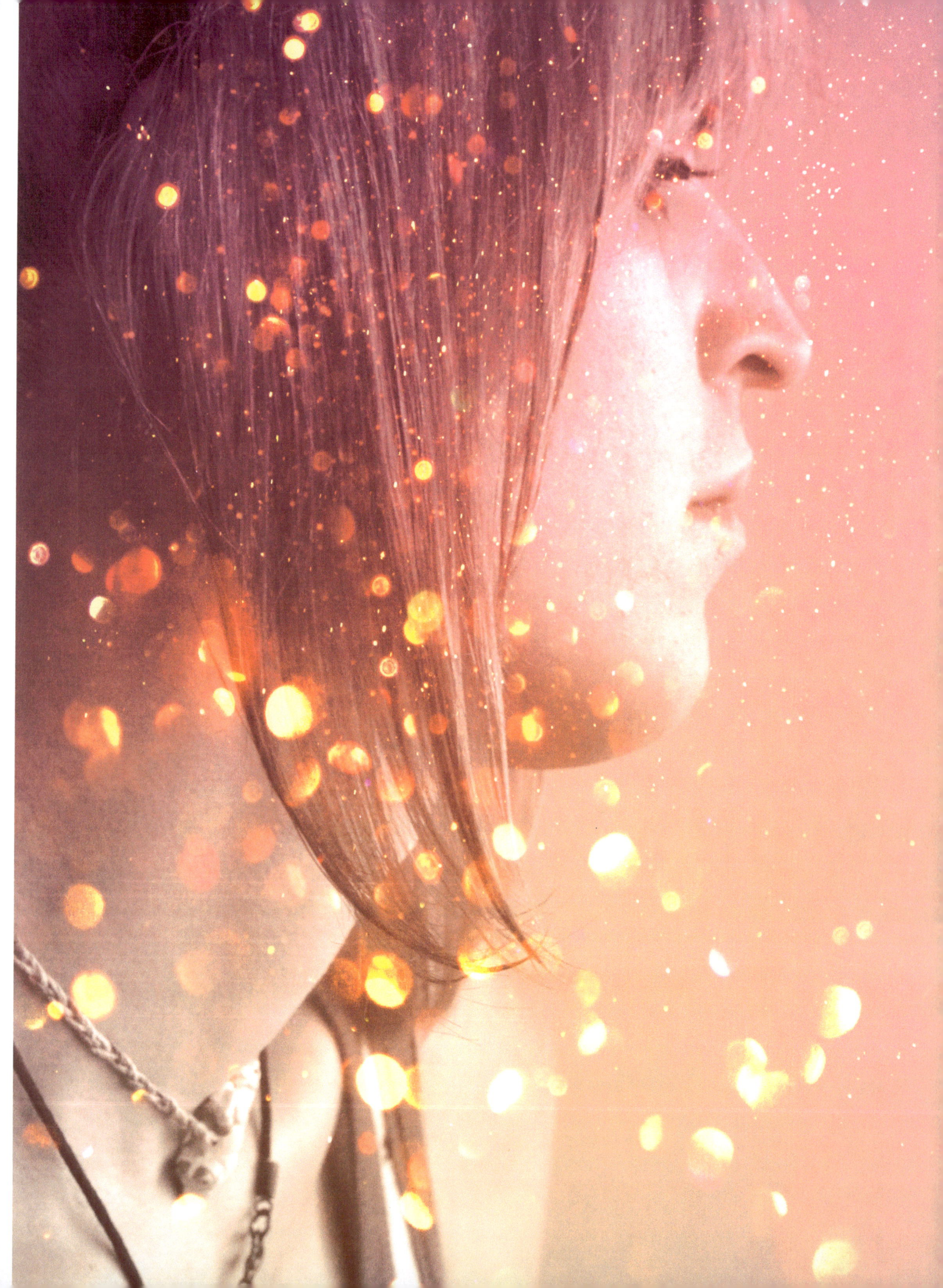

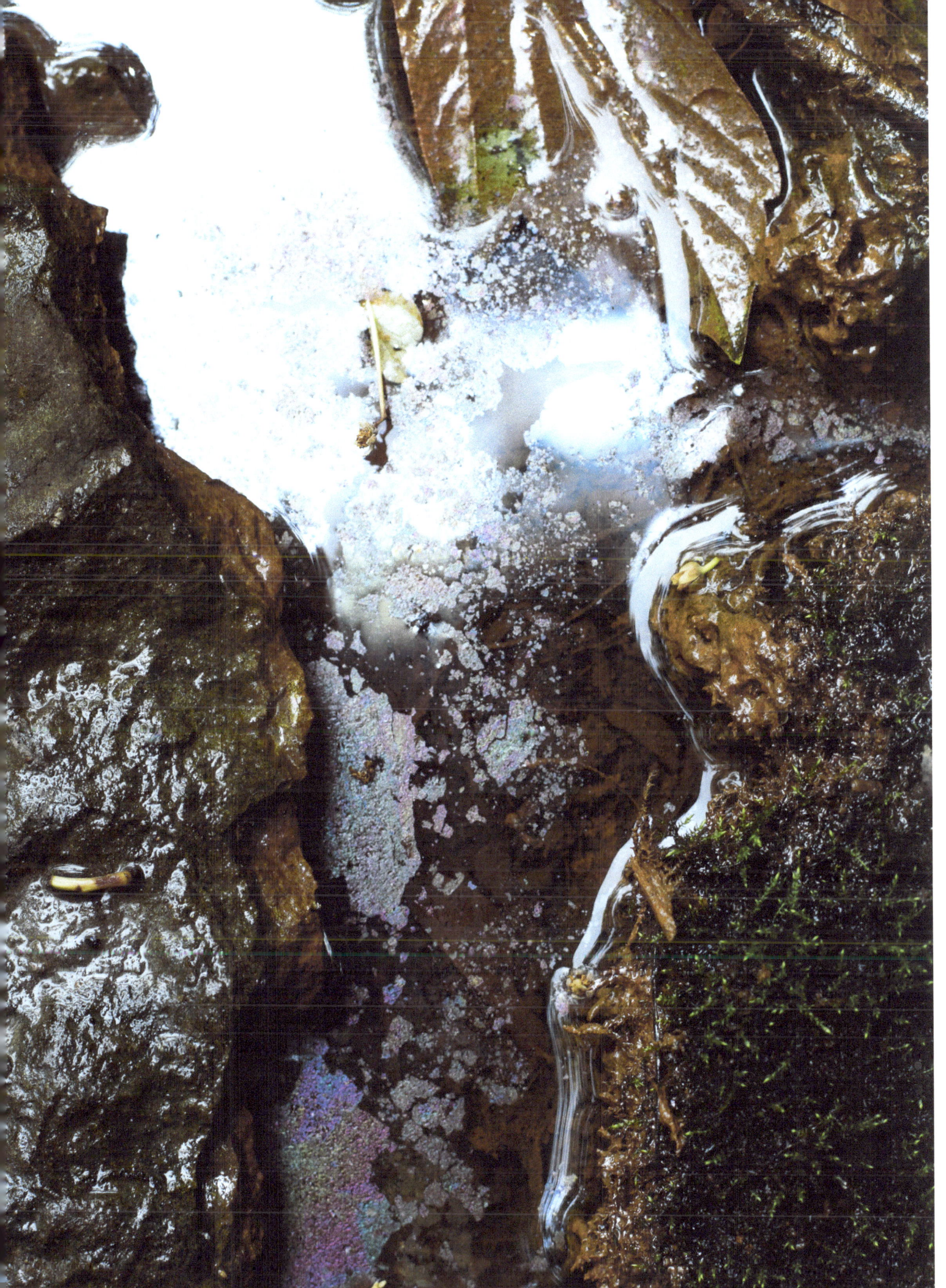

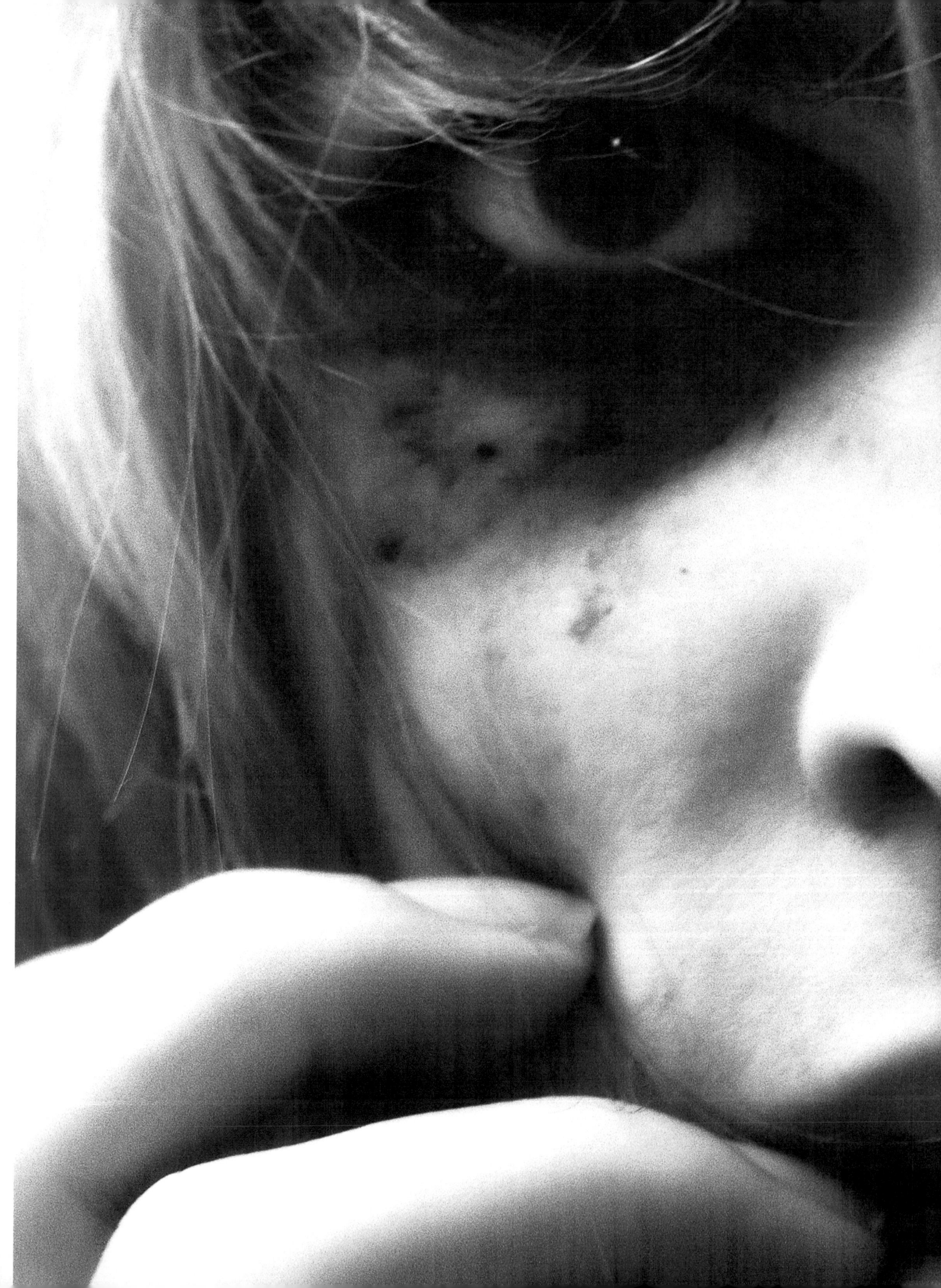

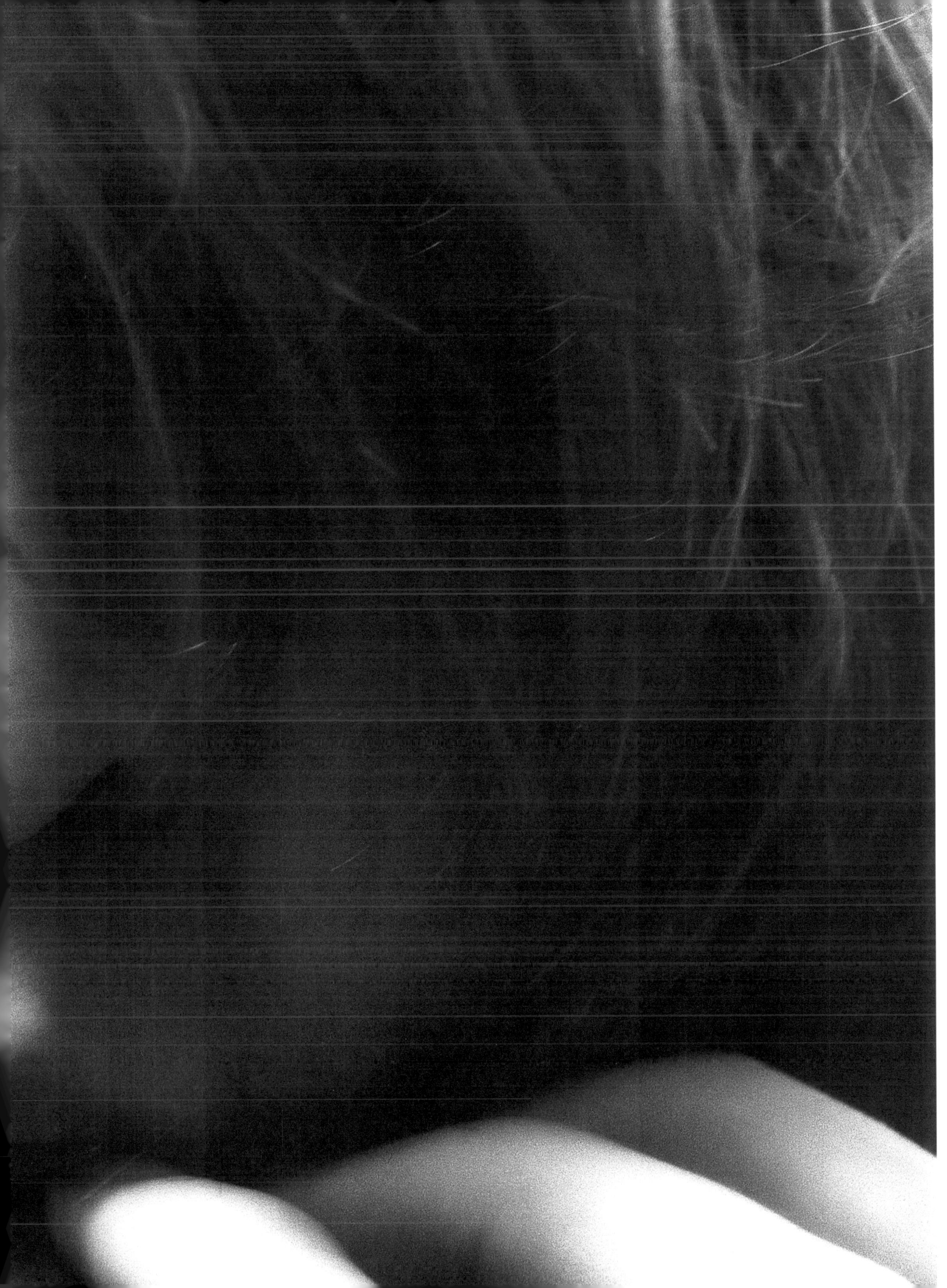

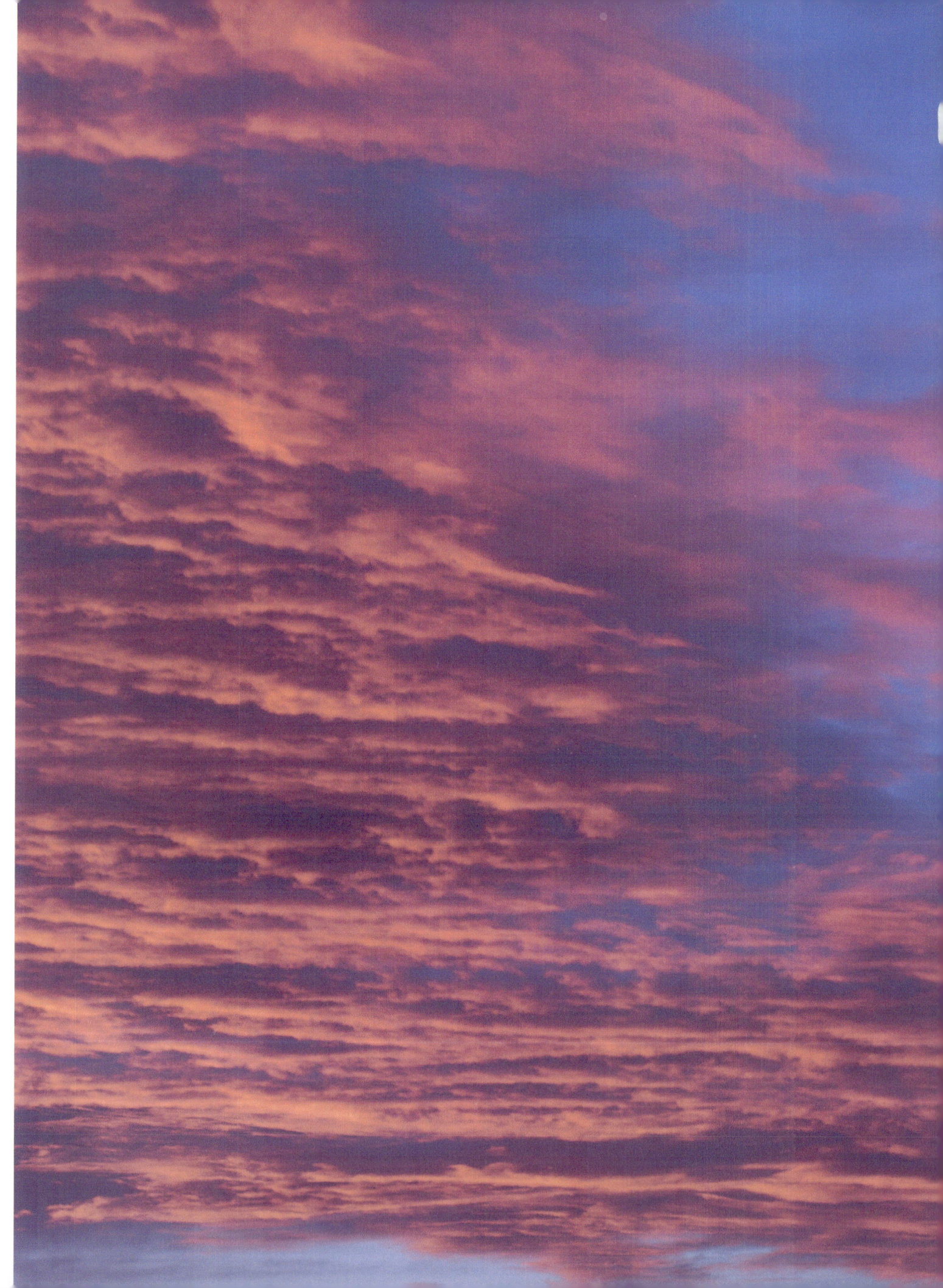

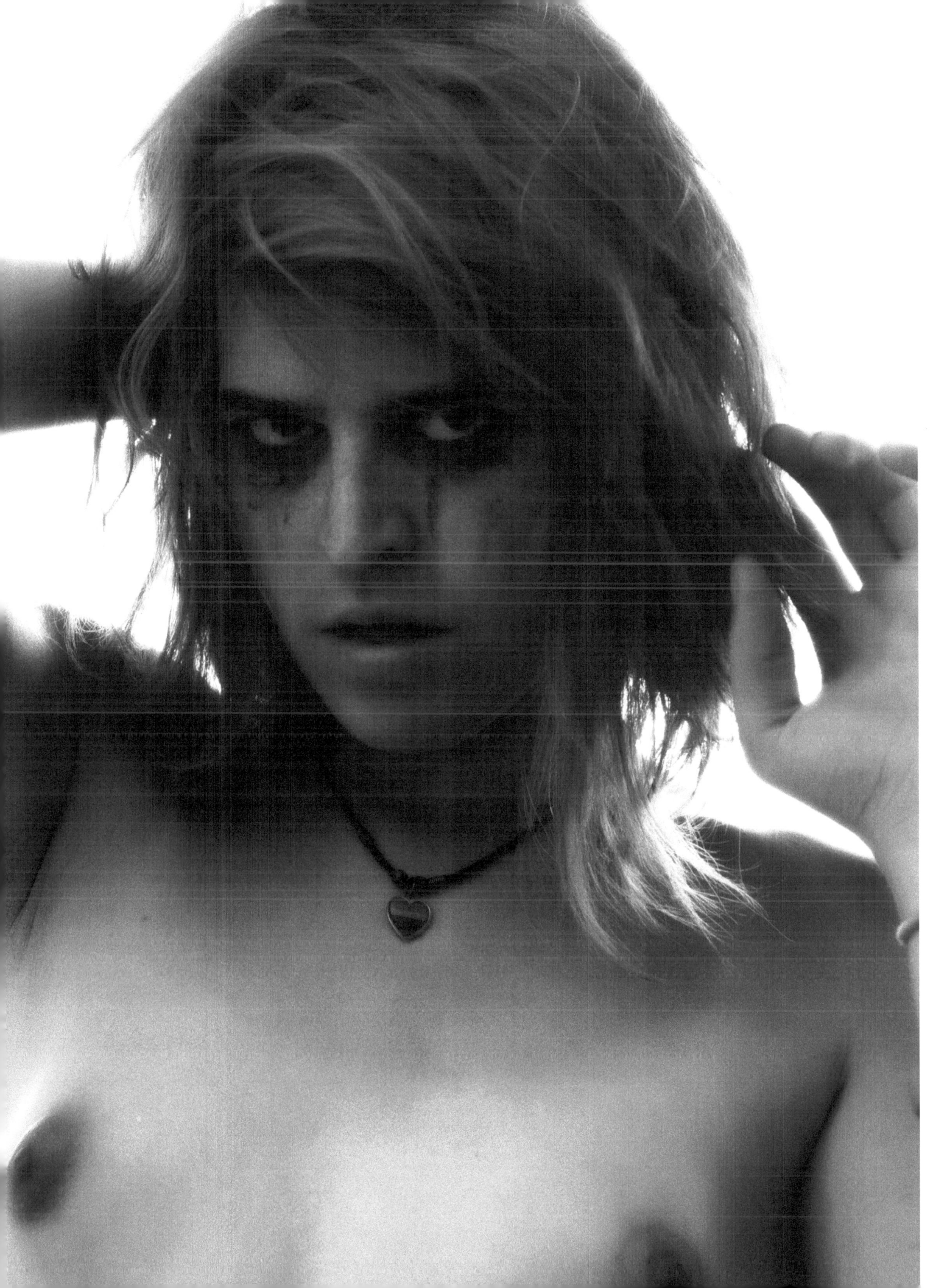

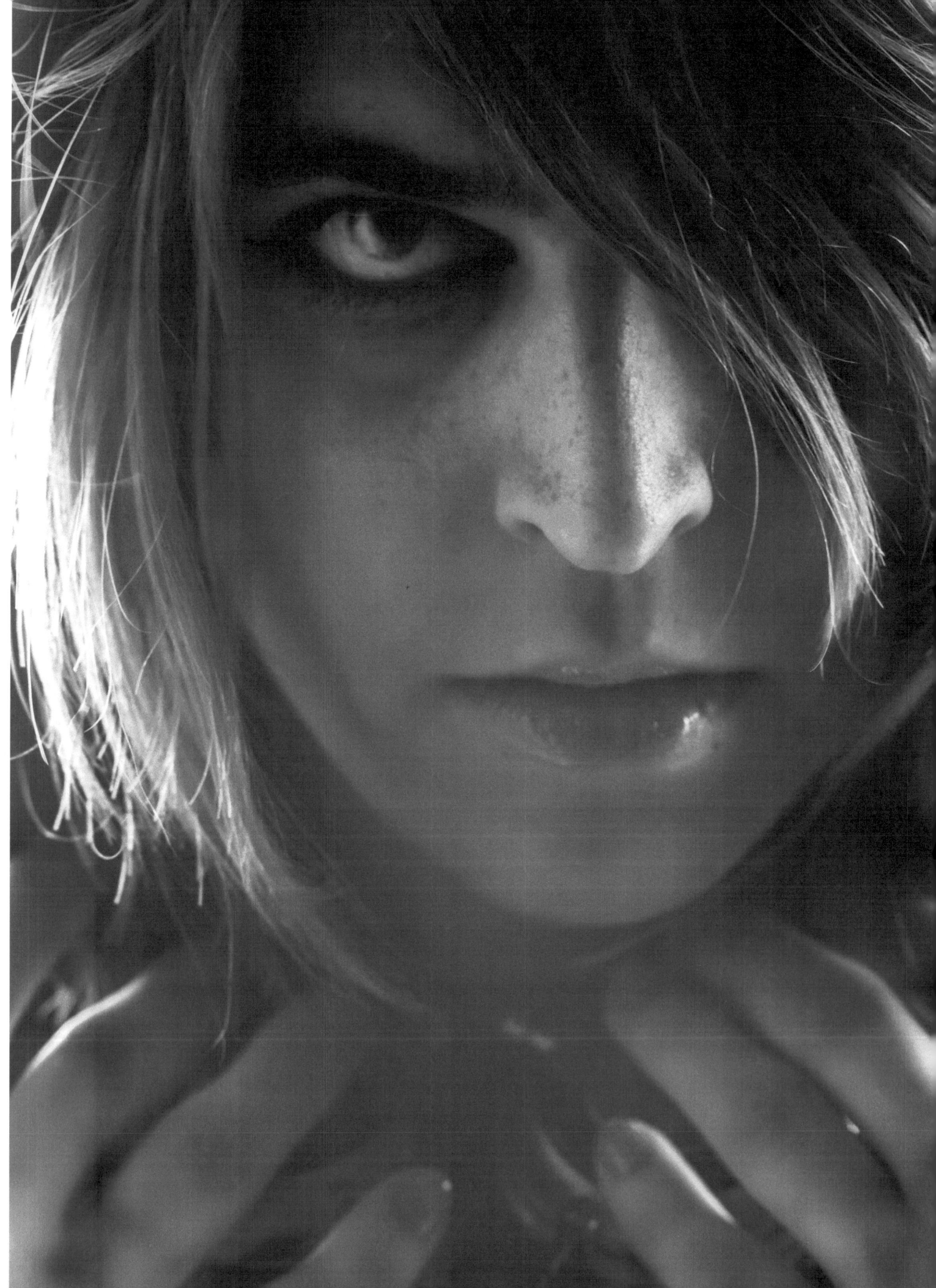

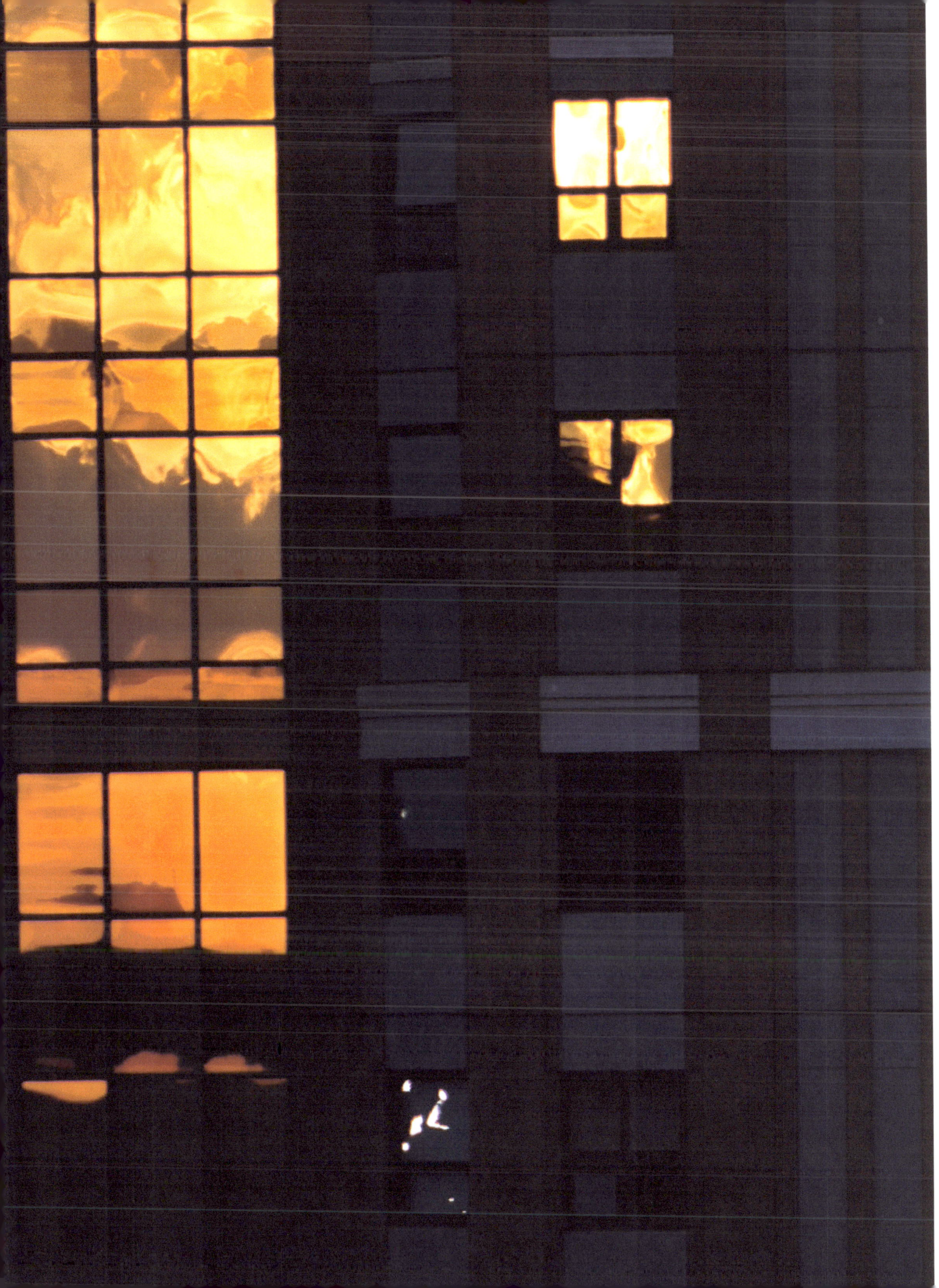

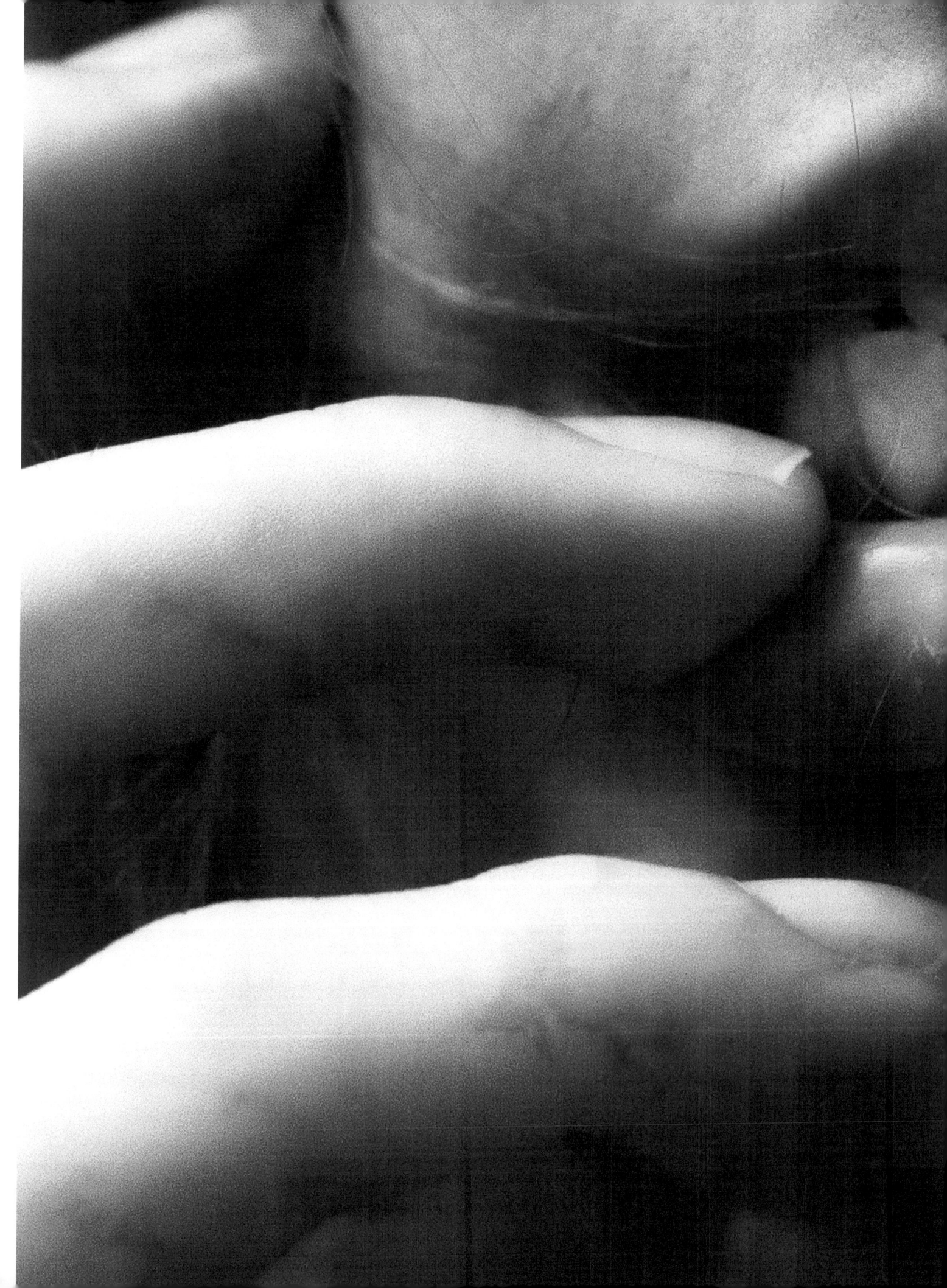

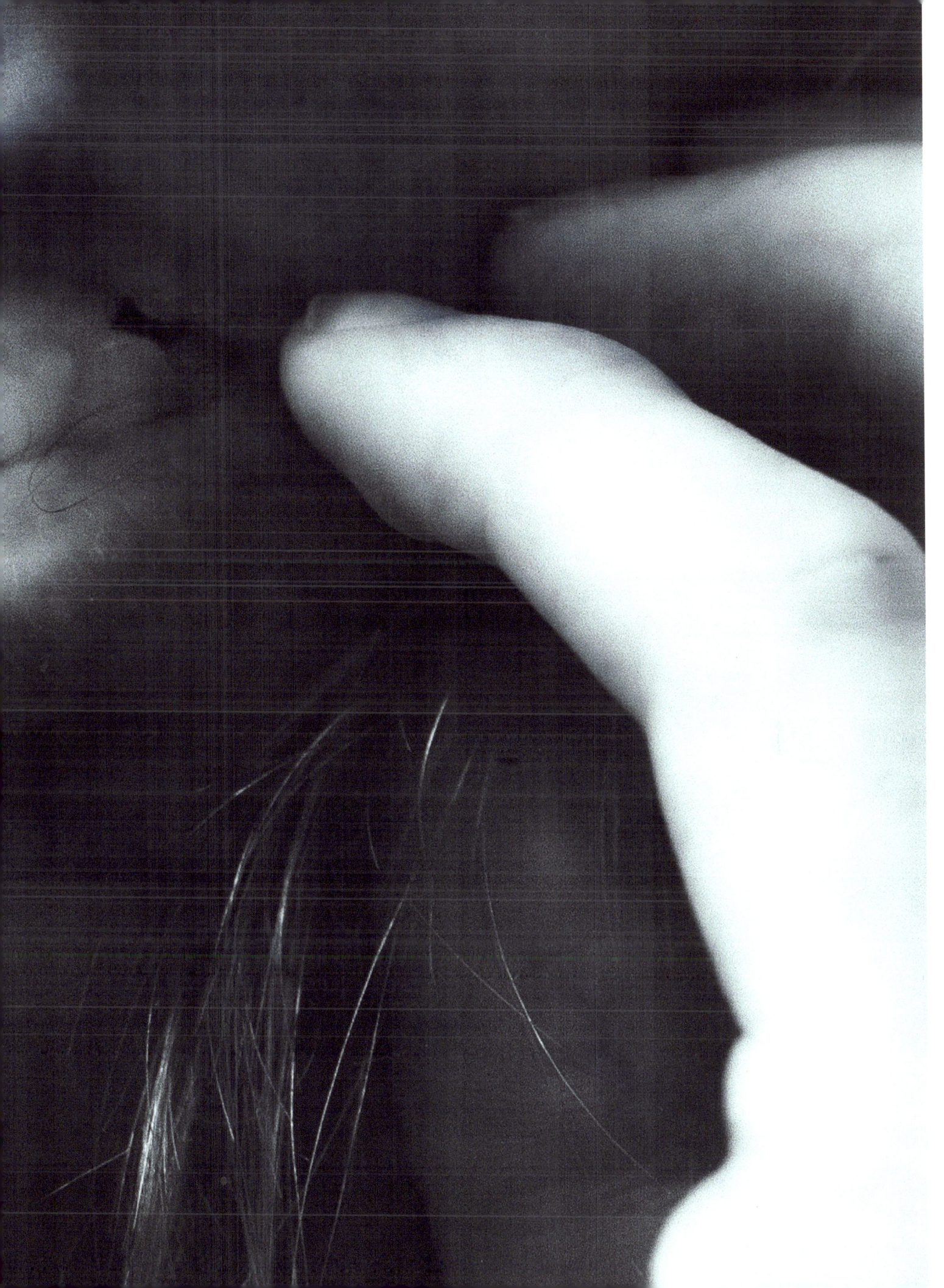

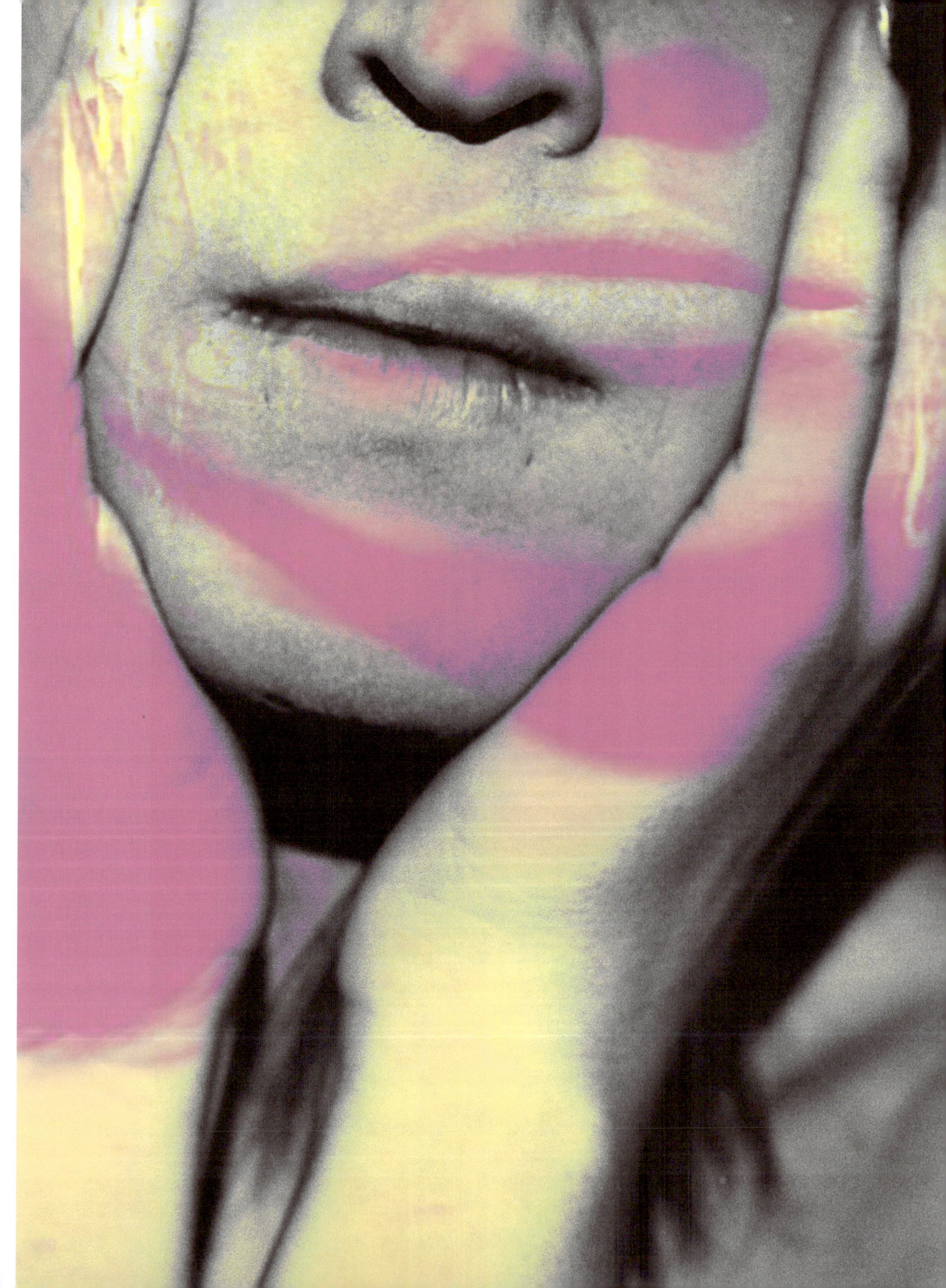

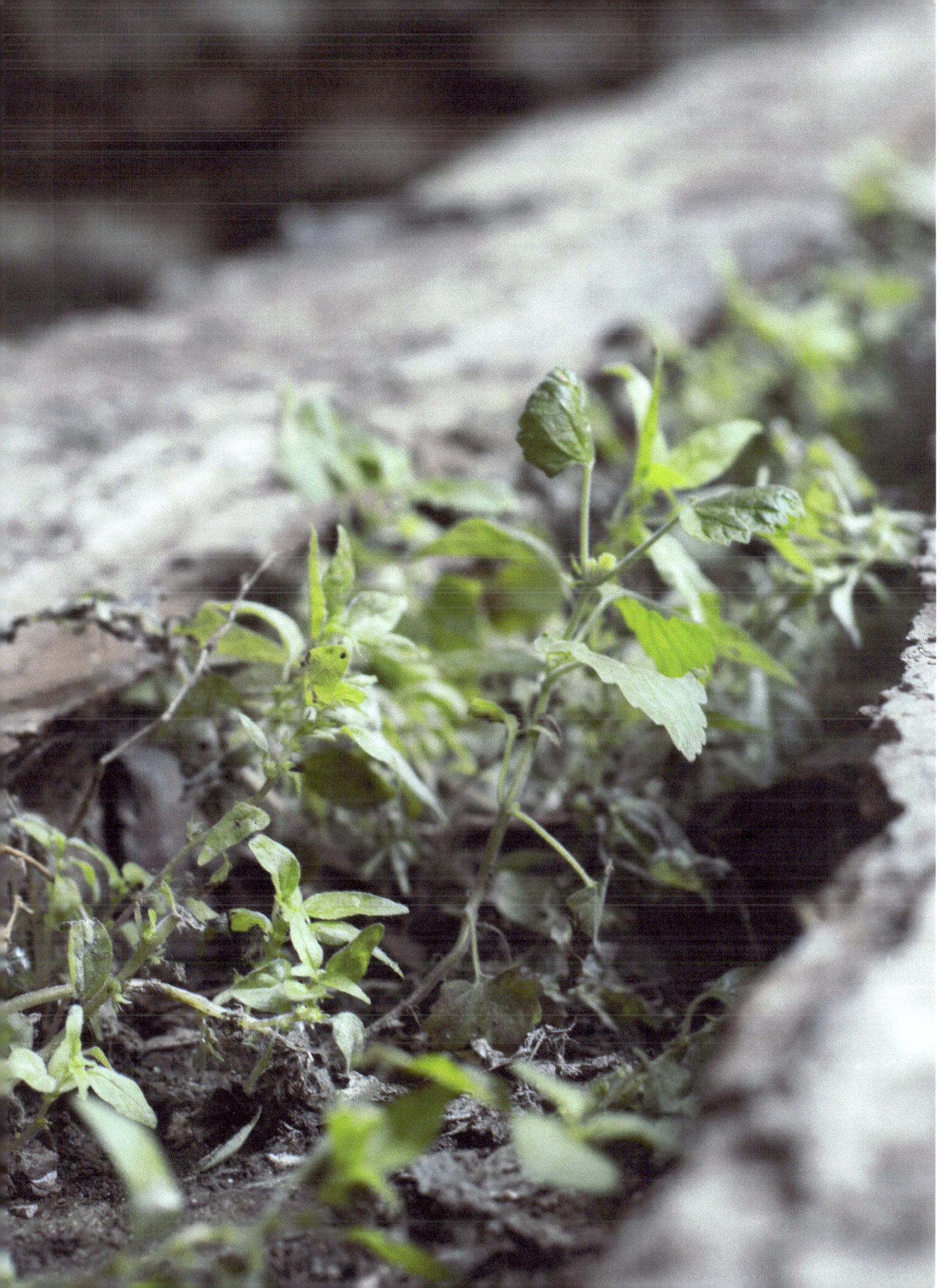

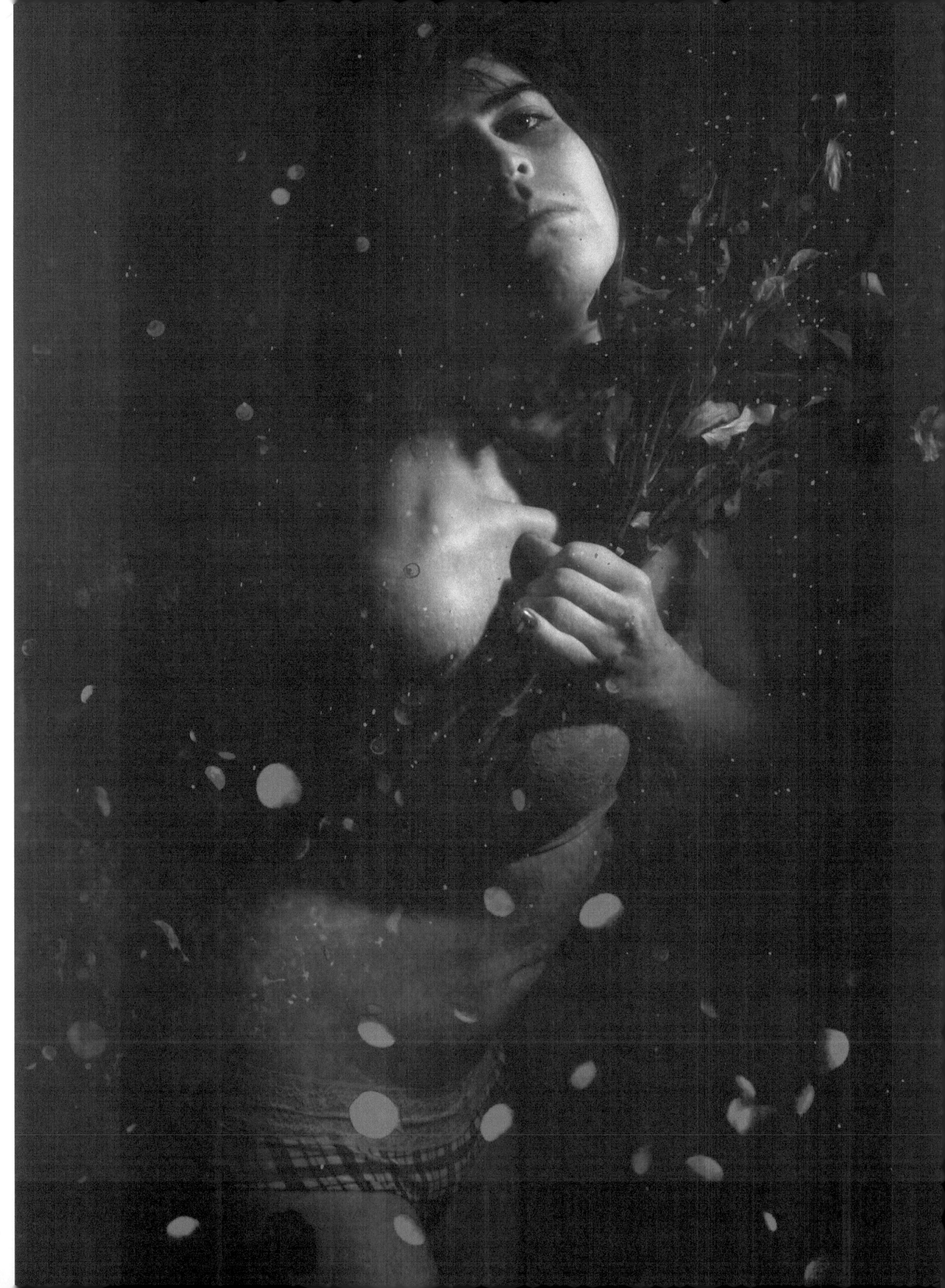

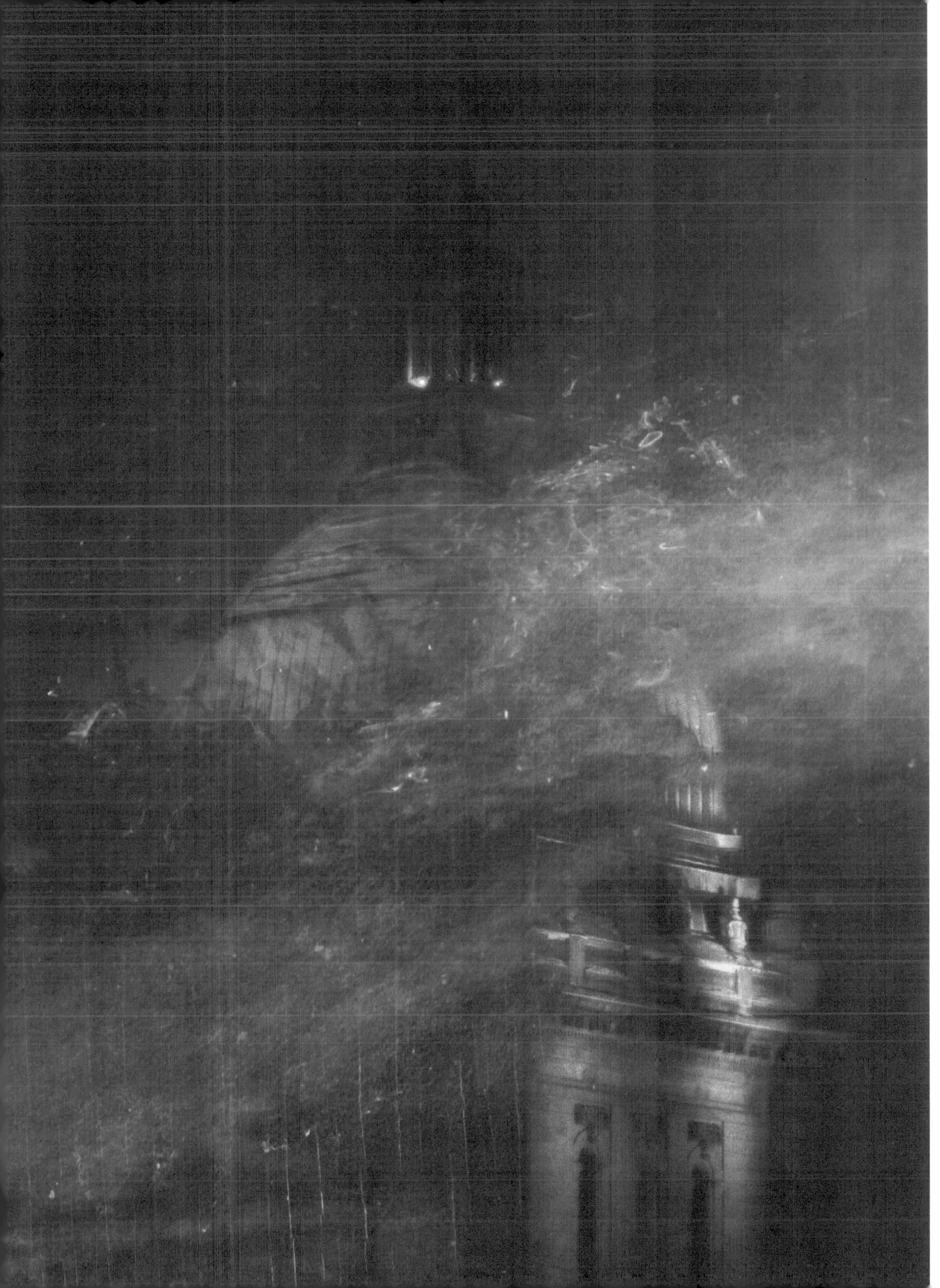

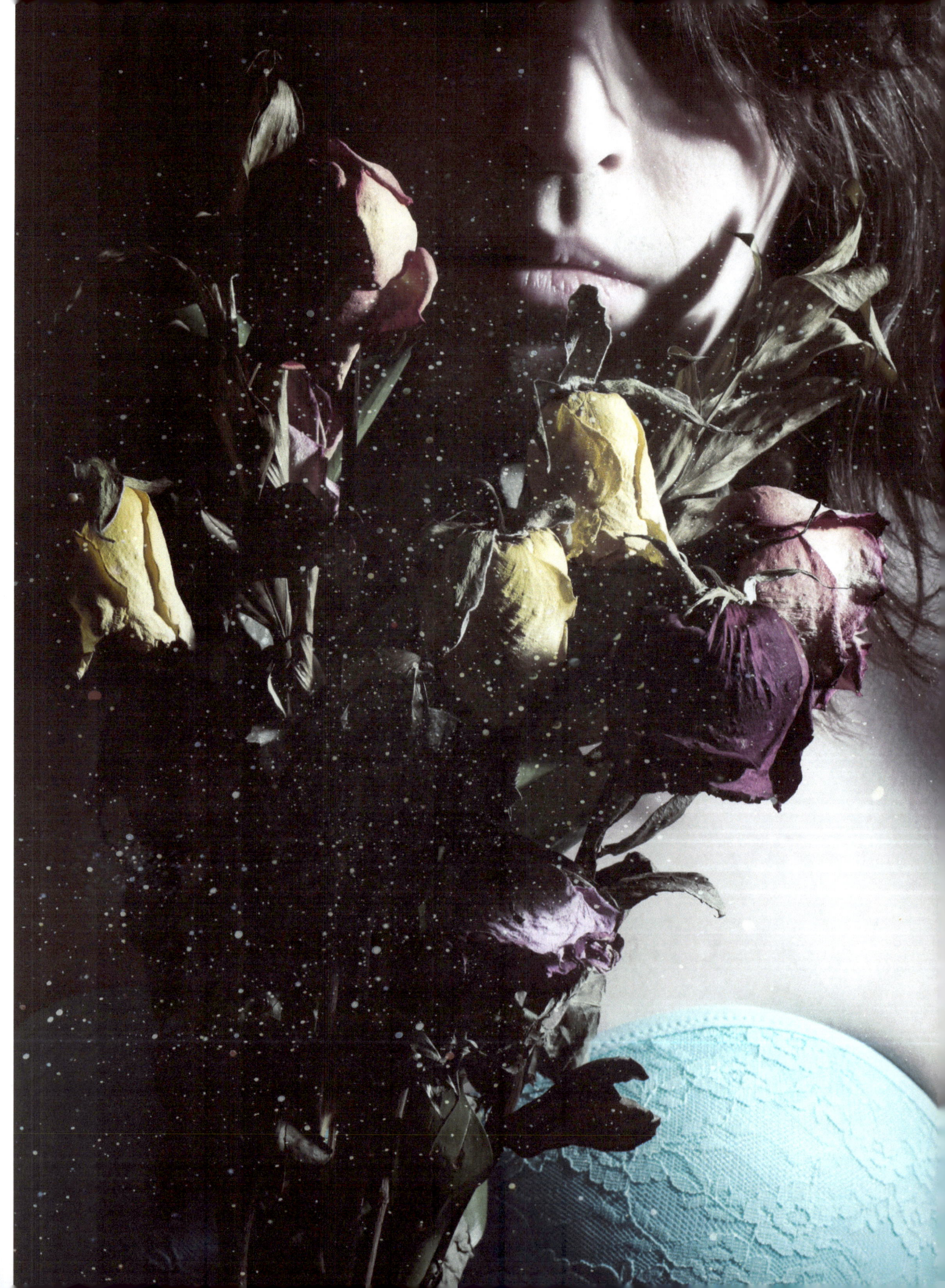

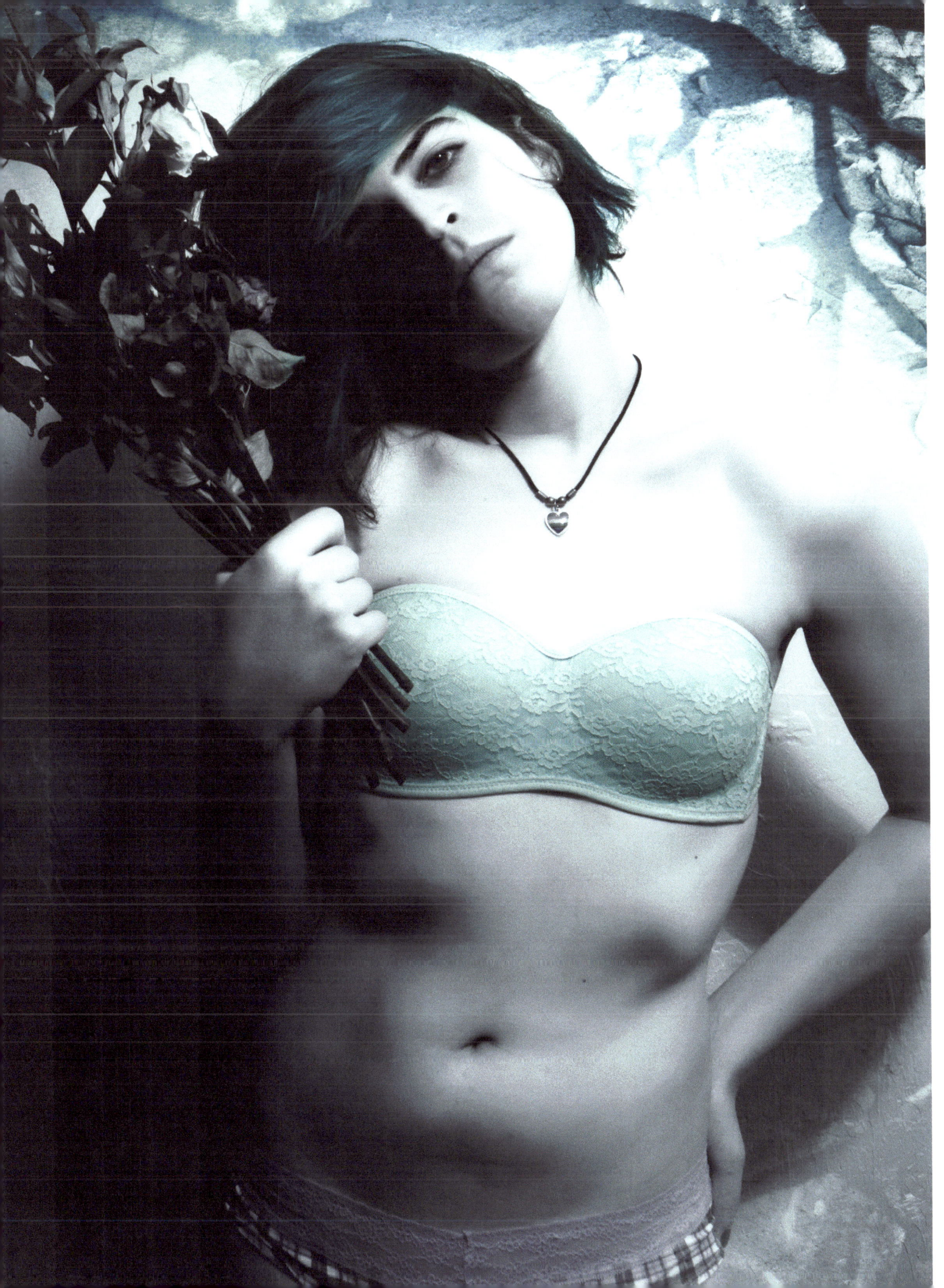

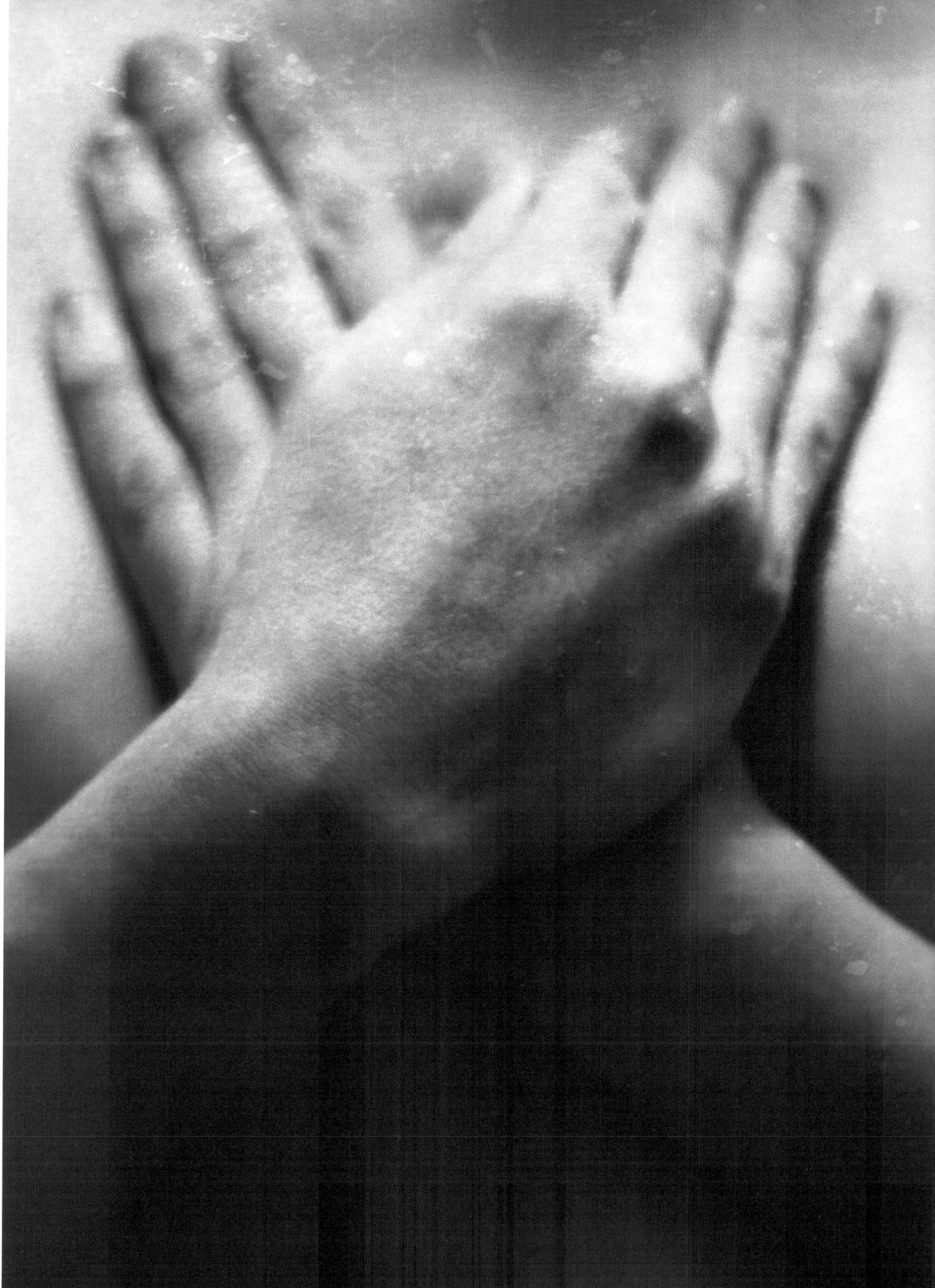